INVENTIONS AND DISCOVERY

Johann Gutenberg
— and the —
Printing Press

by Kay Melchisedech Olson

illustrated by Tod Smith

Consultant:
Eric White, PhD
Curator of Special Collections
Bridwell Library, Southern Methodist University
Dallas, Texas

Capstone
press®
Mankato, Minnesota

Graphic Library is published by Capstone Press,
1710 Roe Crest Drive, NorthMankato, Minnesota 56003.
www.capstonepub.com

Library of Congress Cataloging-in-Publication Data
Olson, Kay Melchisedech.
Johann Gutenberg and the printing press/ by Kay Melchisedech Olson; illustrated by Tod Smith.
p. cm.—(Graphic library. Inventions and discovery)
Includes bibliographical references and index.
ISBN-13: 978-0-7368-6482-4 (hardcover)
ISBN-10: 0-7368-6482-2 (hardcover)
ISBN-13: 978-0-7368-9644-3 (softcover pbk.)
ISBN-10: 0-7368-9644-9 (softcover pbk.)
1. Gutenberg, Johann, 1397?–1468—Juvenile literature. 2. Printers—Germany—Biography—Juvenile literature. 3. Printing—History—Origin and antecedents—Juvenile literature. 4. Books—History—Juvenile literature. I. Smith, Tod, ill. II. Title. III. Series.
Z126.Z7O47 2007
686'.1092—dc22 2006008177

Summary: In graphic novel format, tells the story of Johann Gutenberg and the invention of the printing press.

Designers
Jason Knudson and Juliette Peters

Colorist
Brent Schoonover

Editor
Donald Lemke

Printed in the United States 5904

Table of Contents

Chapter 1

Hand-Copied Books

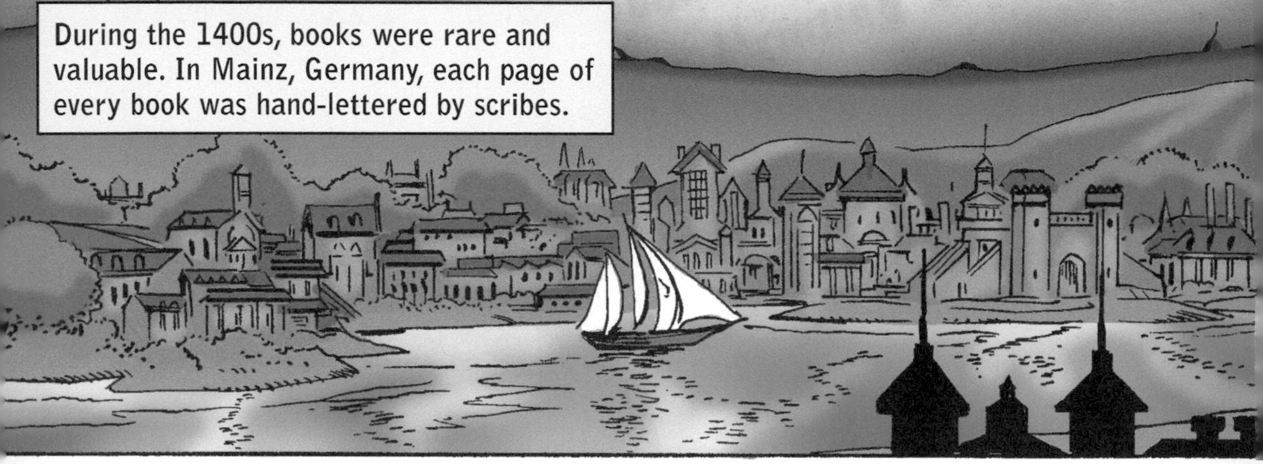
During the 1400s, books were rare and valuable. In Mainz, Germany, each page of every book was hand-lettered by scribes.

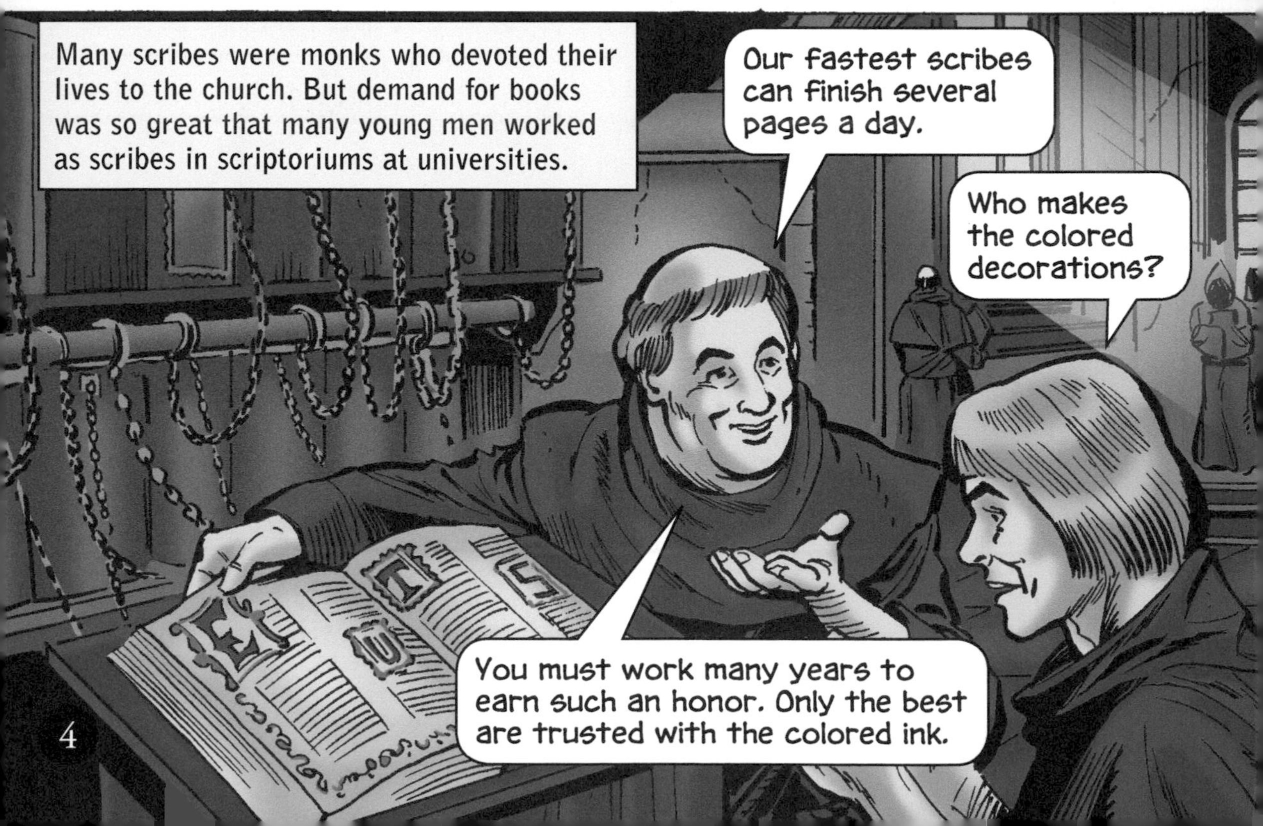
Many scribes were monks who devoted their lives to the church. But demand for books was so great that many young men worked as scribes in scriptoriums at universities.
Our fastest scribes can finish several pages a day.
Who makes the colored decorations?
You must work many years to earn such an honor. Only the best are trusted with the colored ink.

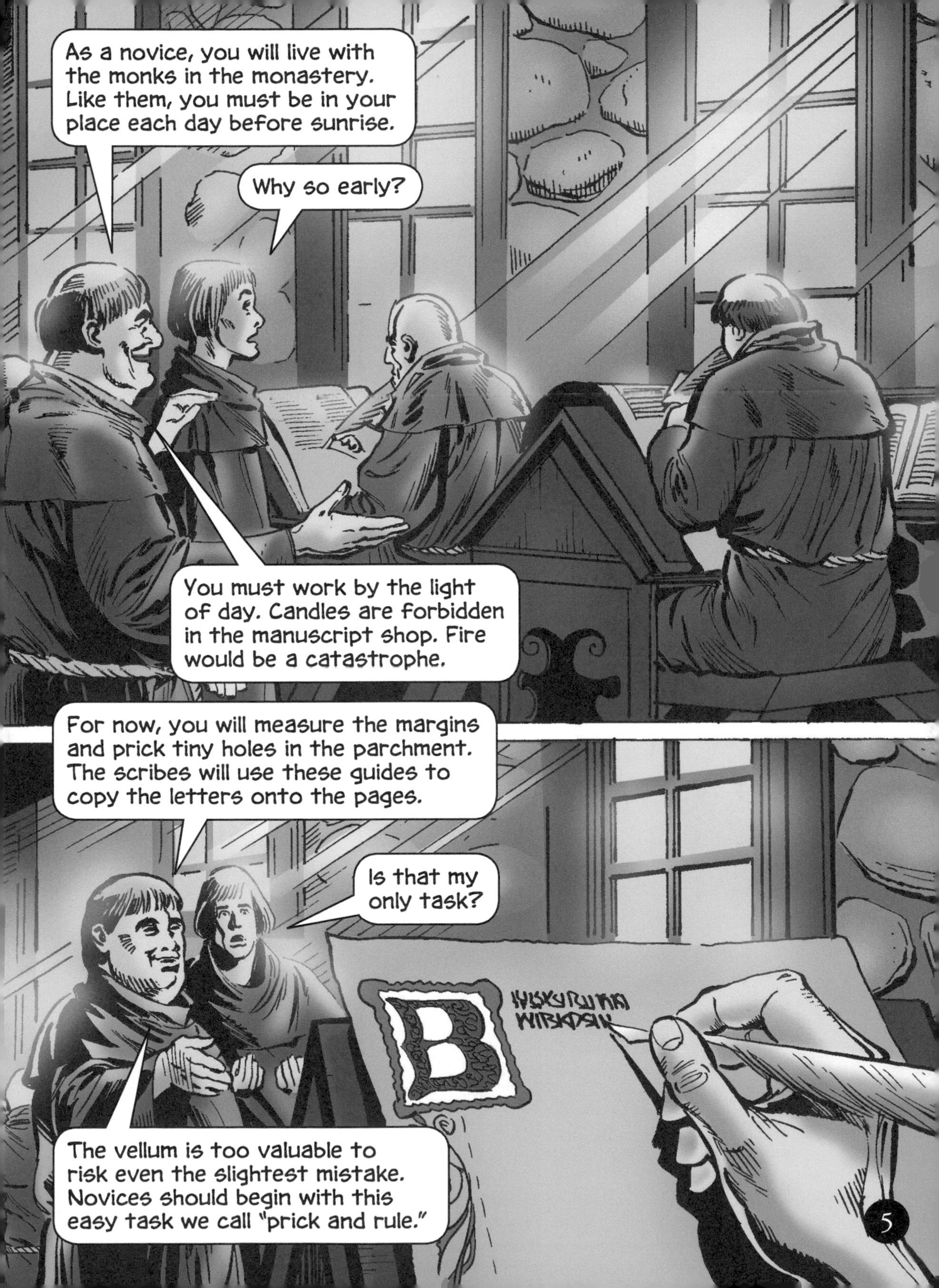
As a novice, you will live with the monks in the monastery. Like them, you must be in your place each day before sunrise.
Why so early?
You must work by the light of day. Candles are forbidden in the manuscript shop. Fire would be a catastrophe.
For now, you will measure the margins and prick tiny holes in the parchment. The scribes will use these guides to copy the letters onto the pages.
Is that my only task?
The vellum is too valuable to risk even the slightest mistake. Novices should begin with this easy task we call "prick and rule."

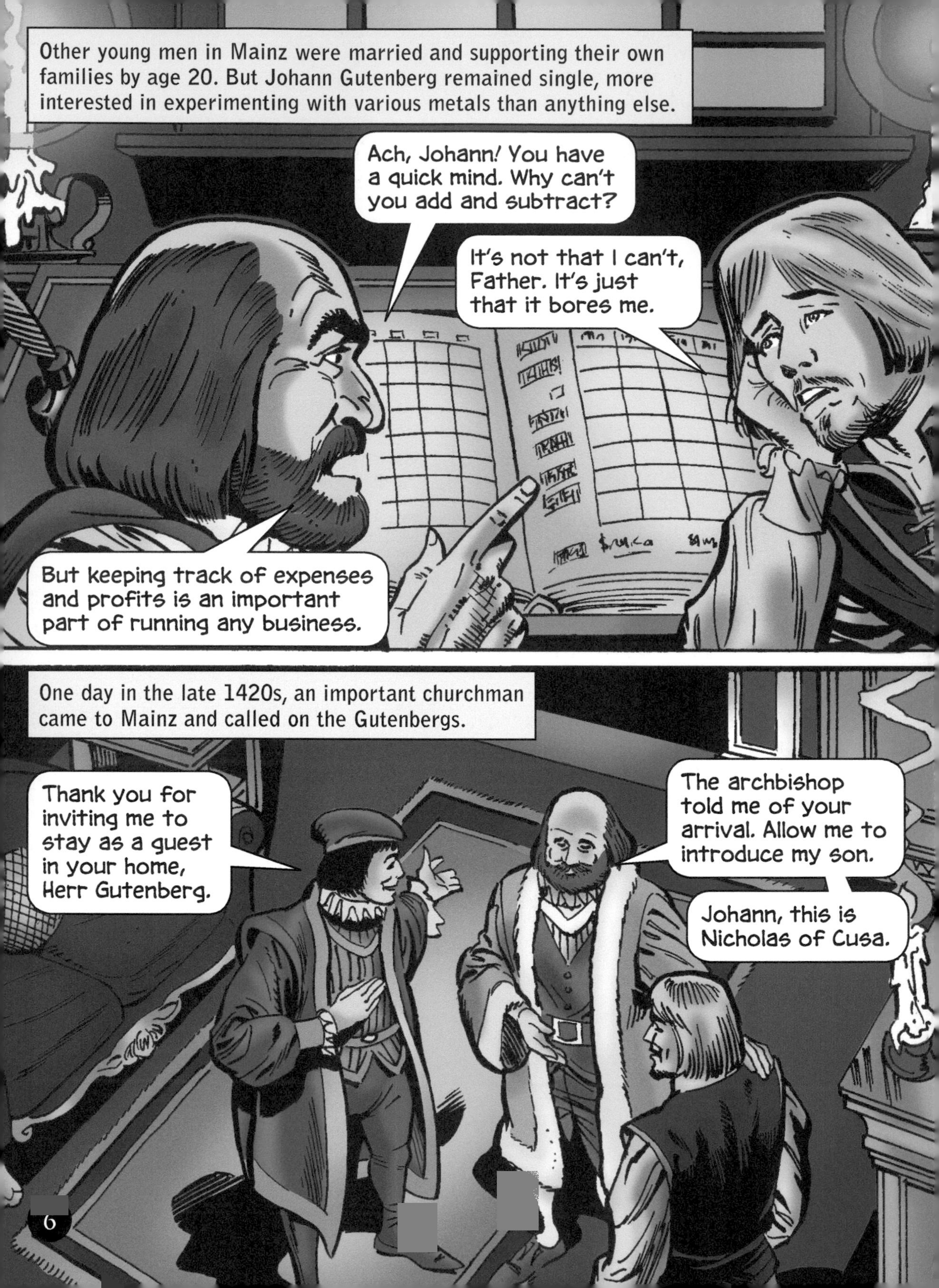

Other young men in Mainz were married and supporting their own families by age 20. But Johann Gutenberg remained single, more interested in experimenting with various metals than anything else.
Ach, Johann! You have a quick mind. Why can't you add and subtract?
It's not that I can't, Father. It's just that it bores me.
But keeping track of expenses and profits is an important part of running any business.
One day in the late 1420s, an important churchman came to Mainz and called on the Gutenbergs.
Thank you for inviting me to stay as a guest in your home, Herr Gutenberg.
The archbishop told me of your arrival. Allow me to introduce my son.
Johann, this is Nicholas of Cusa.

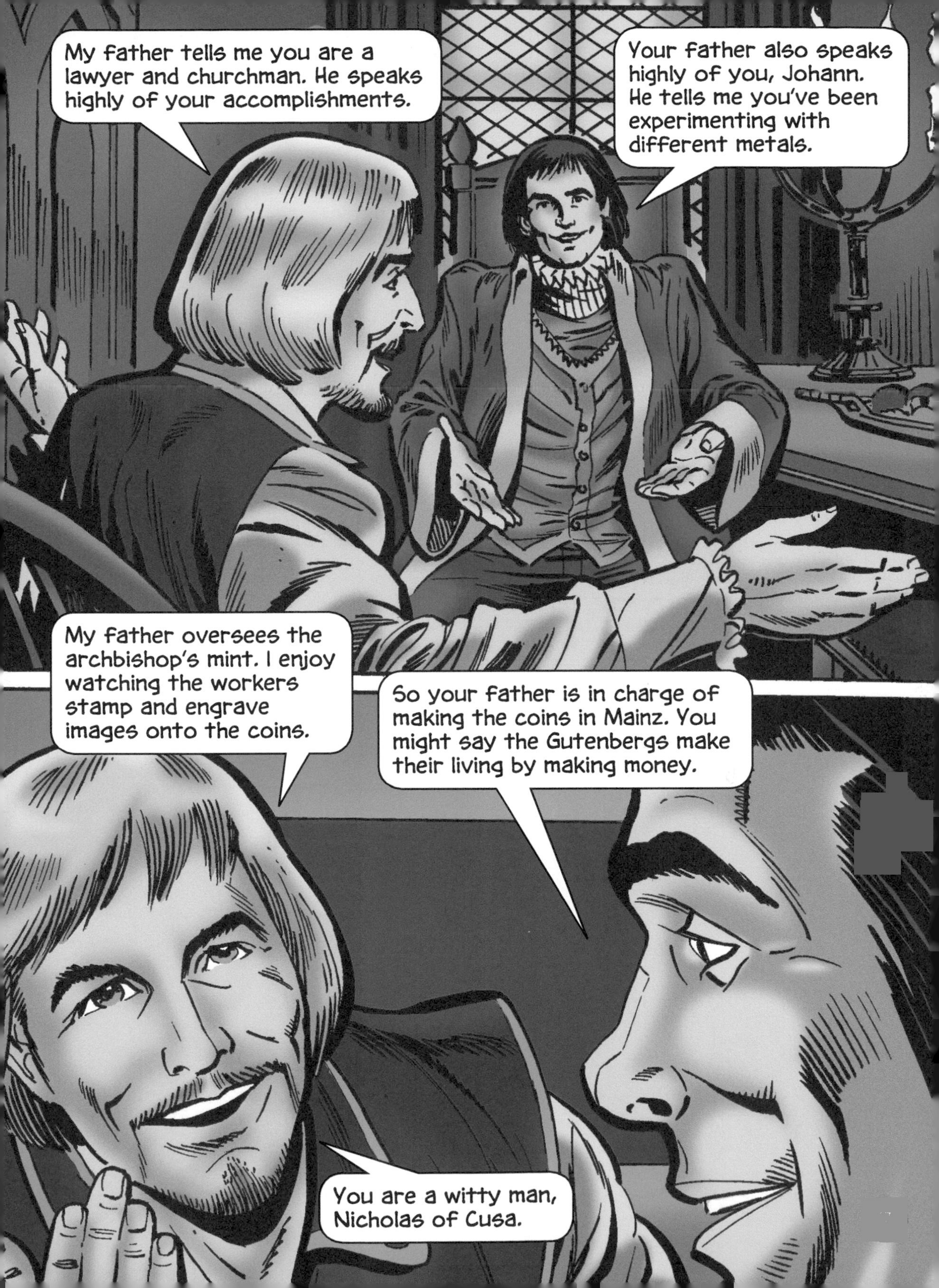
My father tells me you are a lawyer and churchman. He speaks highly of your accomplishments.
Your father also speaks highly of you, Johann. He tells me you've been experimenting with different metals.
My father oversees the archbishop's mint. I enjoy watching the workers stamp and engrave images onto the coins.
So your father is in charge of making the coins in Mainz. You might say the Gutenbergs make their living by making money.
You are a witty man, Nicholas of Cusa.

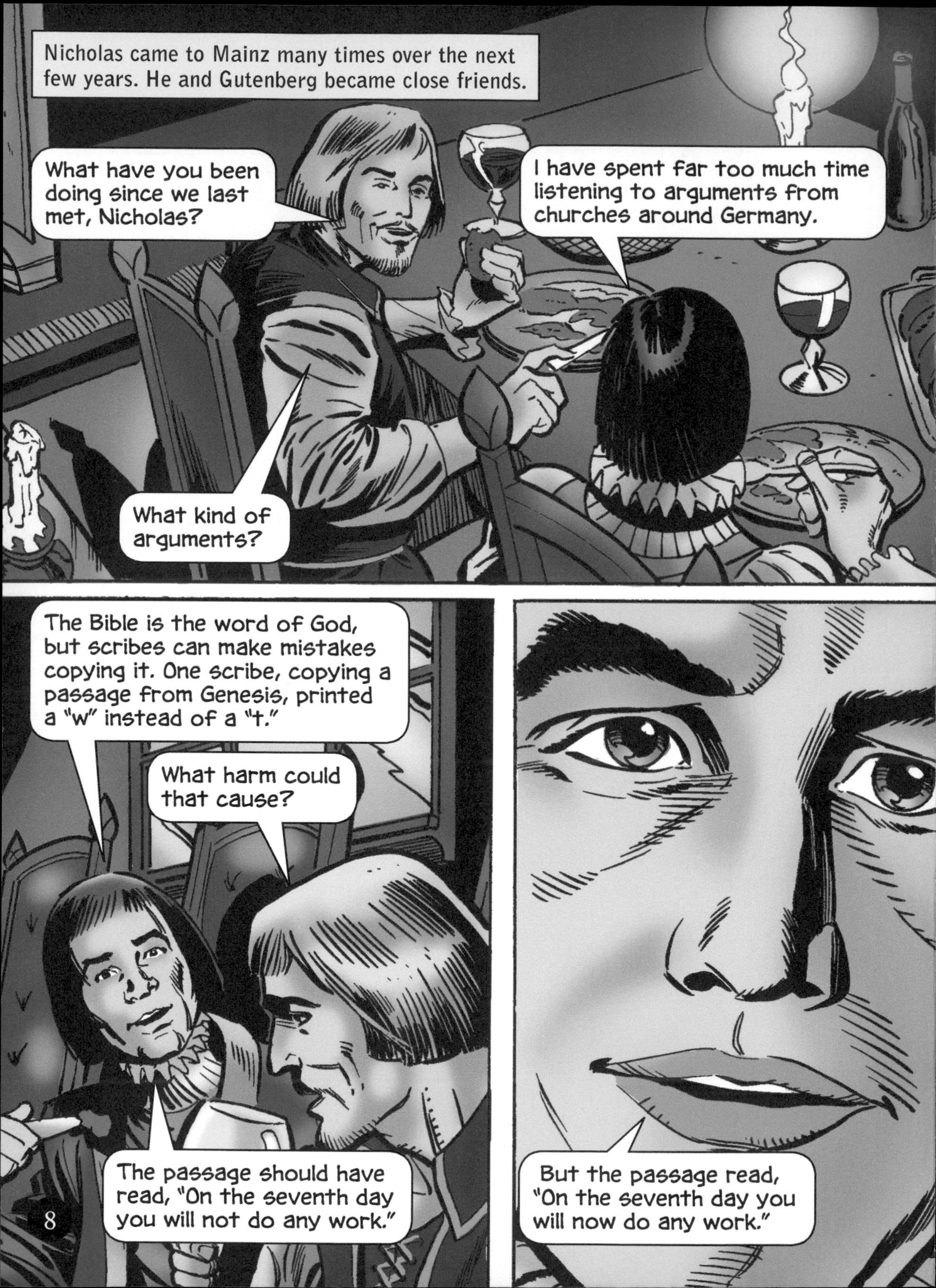
Nicholas came to Mainz many times over the next few years. He and Gutenberg became close friends.
What have you been doing since we last met, Nicholas?
I have spent far too much time listening to arguments from churches around Germany.
What kind of arguments?
The Bible is the word of God, but scribes can make mistakes copying it. One scribe, copying a passage from Genesis, printed a "w" instead of a "t."
What harm could that cause?
The passage should have read, "On the seventh day you will not do any work."
But the passage read, "On the seventh day you will now do any work."

But why would such a little mistake cause arguments?
Members of each church believe their Bible is correct. But no two copies are exactly the same. People argue over whose Bible is the true word of God.

If only someone could find a way to make hundreds of copies of the Bible, each exactly the same. Such a thing would be like a miracle, uniting Christians everywhere.

Chapter 2

A Secret Project

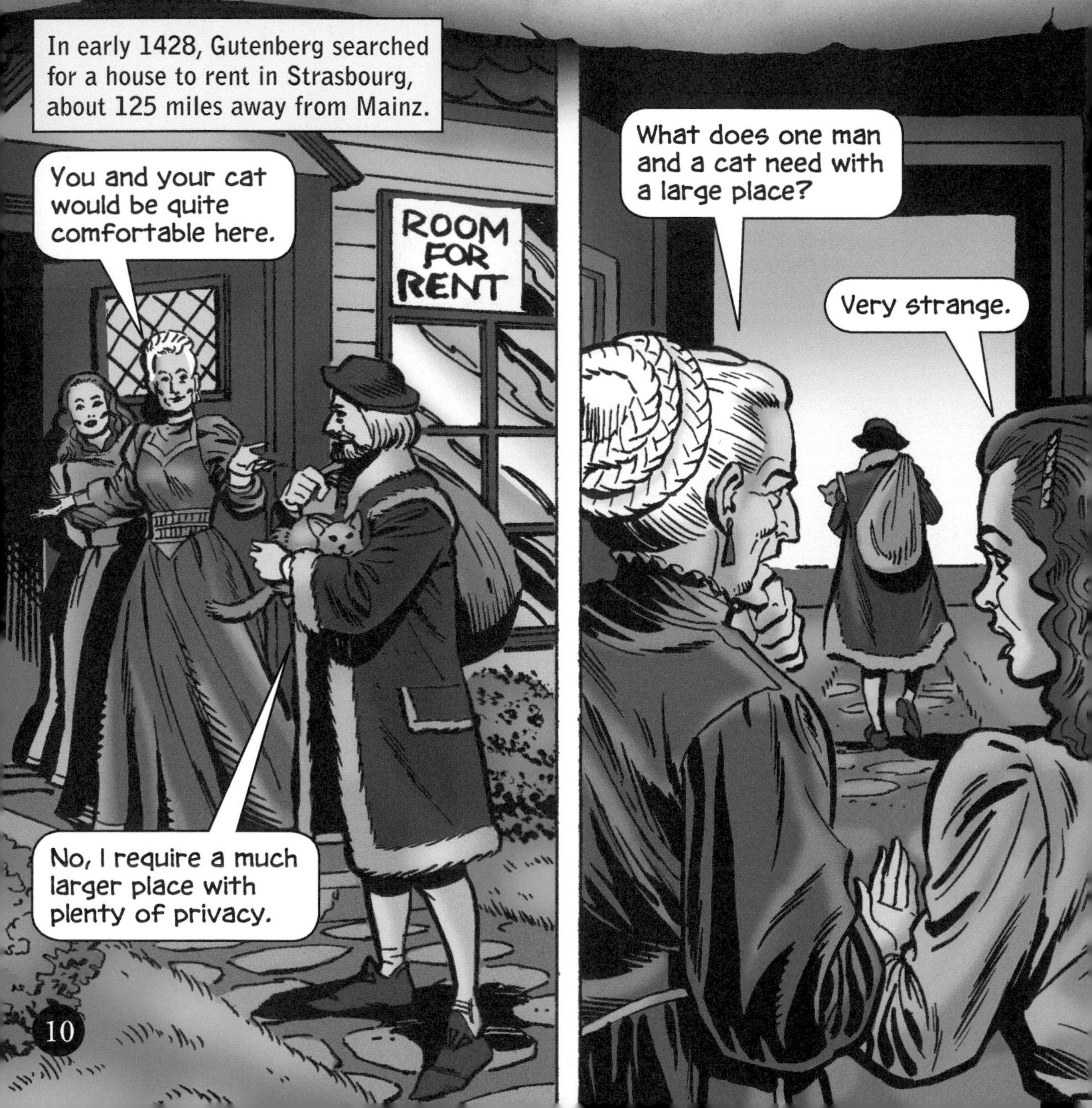
In early 1428, Gutenberg searched for a house to rent in Strasbourg, about 125 miles away from Mainz.
You and your cat would be quite comfortable here.
ROOM FOR RENT
No, I require a much larger place with plenty of privacy.
What does one man and a cat need with a large place?
Very strange.

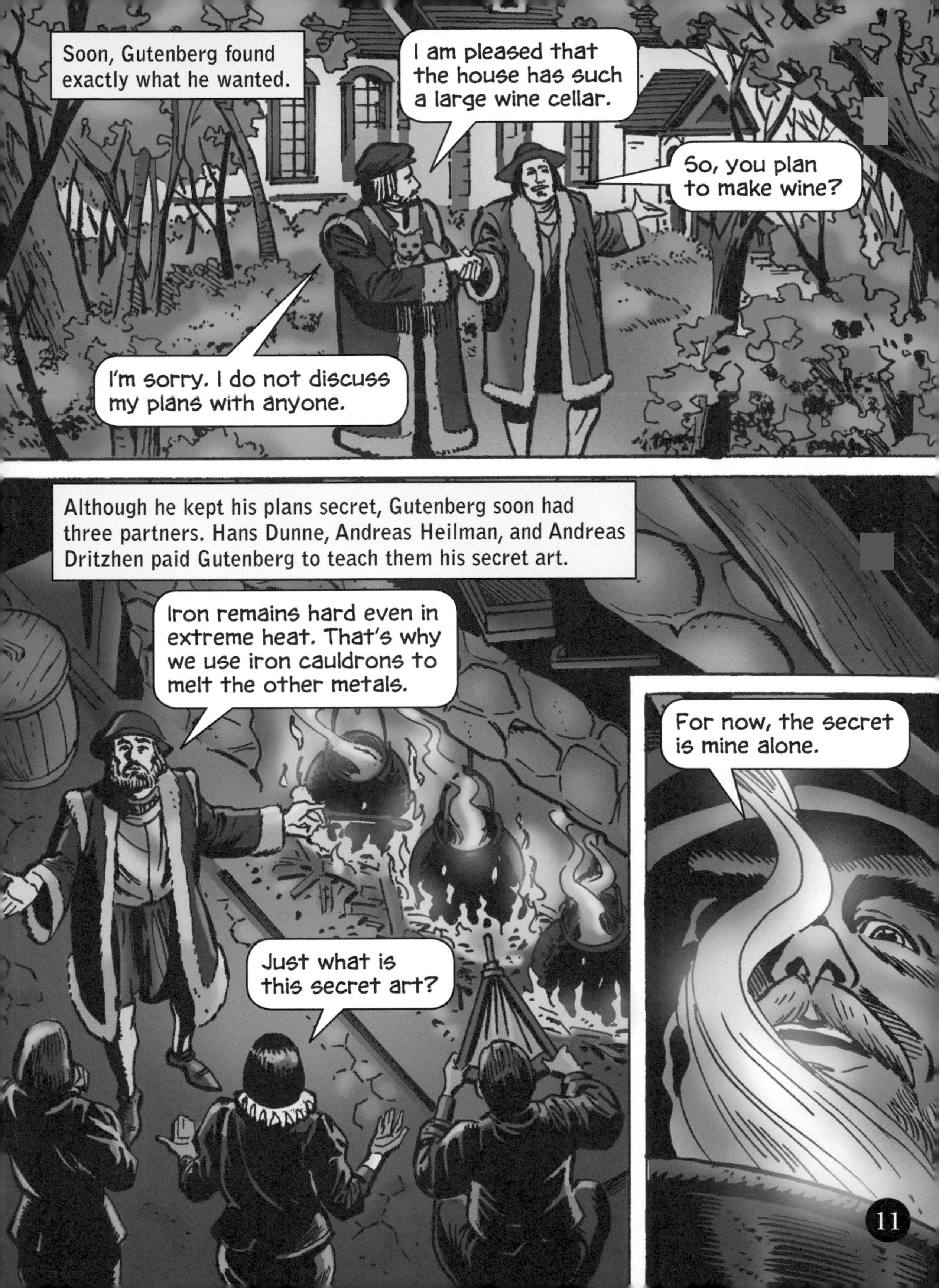
Soon, Gutenberg found exactly what he wanted.
I am pleased that the house has such a large wine cellar.
So, you plan to make wine?
I'm sorry. I do not discuss my plans with anyone.
Although he kept his plans secret, Gutenberg soon had three partners. Hans Dunne, Andreas Heilman, and Andreas Dritzhen paid Gutenberg to teach them his secret art.
Iron remains hard even in extreme heat. That's why we use iron cauldrons to melt the other metals.
Just what is this secret art?
For now, the secret is mine alone.

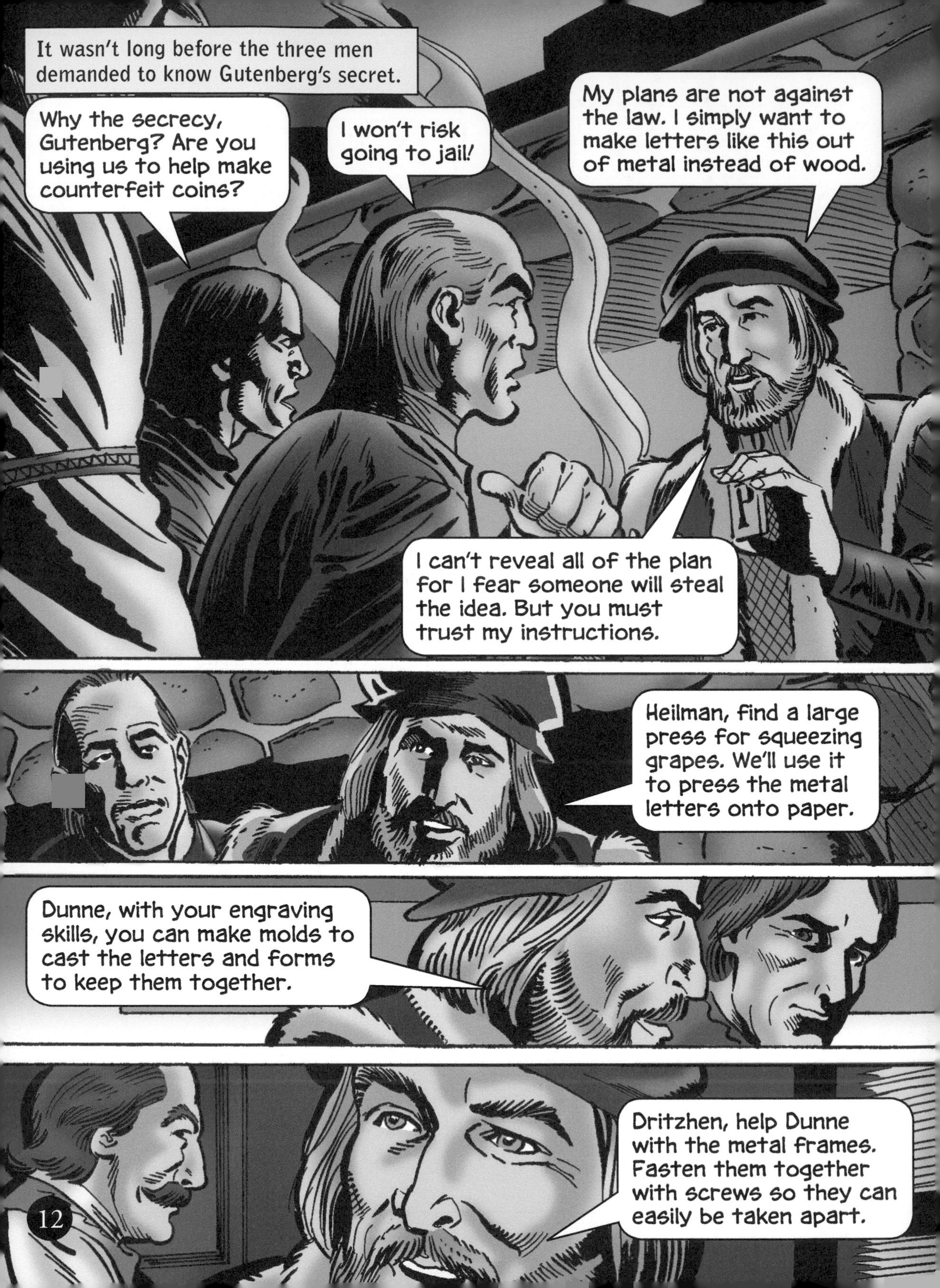
It wasn't long before the three men demanded to know Gutenberg's secret.
Why the secrecy, Gutenberg? Are you using us to help make counterfeit coins?
I won't risk going to jail!
My plans are not against the law. I simply want to make letters like this out of metal instead of wood.
I can't reveal all of the plan for I fear someone will steal the idea. But you must trust my instructions.
Heilman, find a large press for squeezing grapes. We'll use it to press the metal letters onto paper.
Dunne, with your engraving skills, you can make molds to cast the letters and forms to keep them together.
Dritzhen, help Dunne with the metal frames. Fasten them together with screws so they can easily be taken apart.

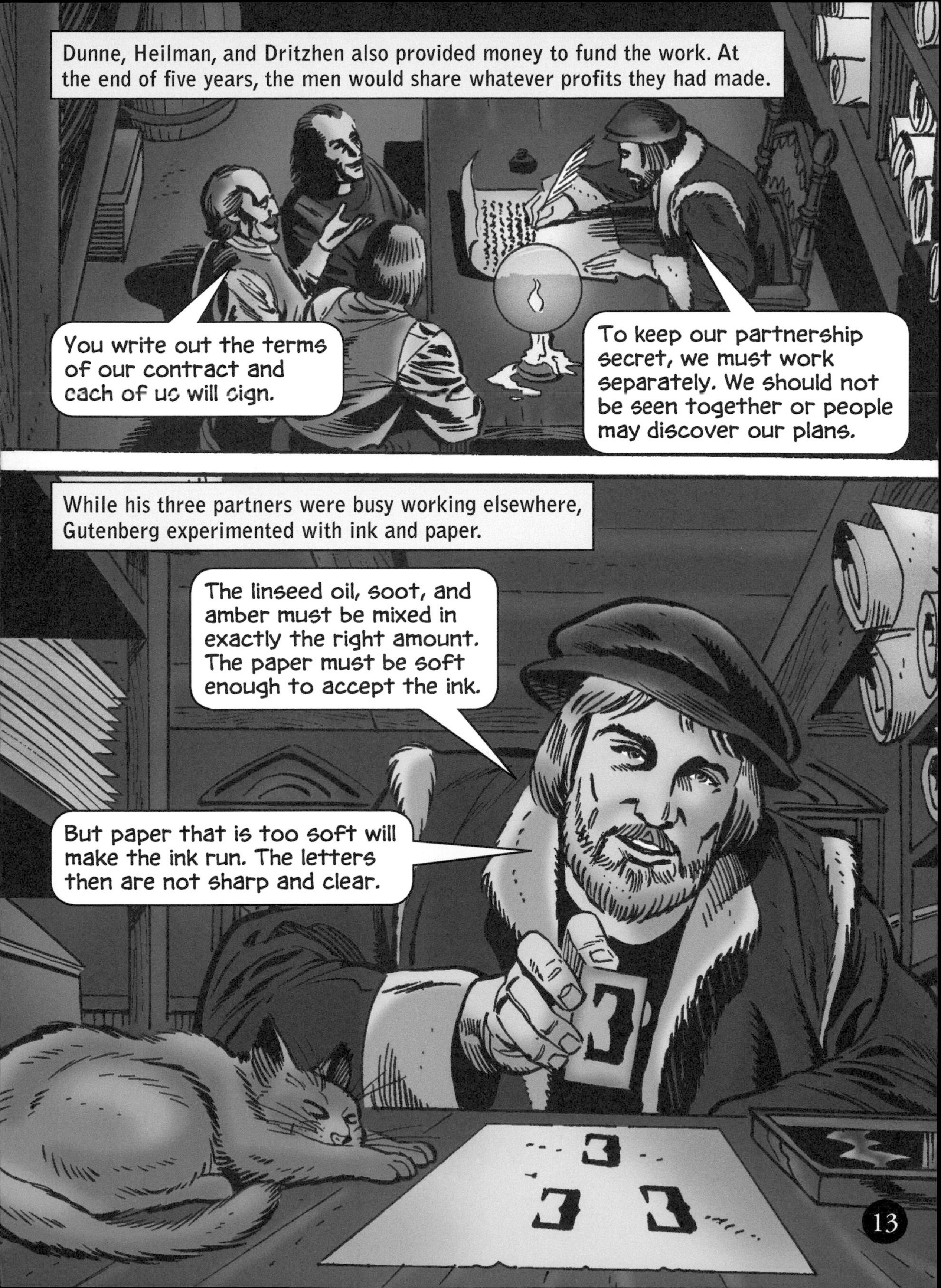
Dunne, Heilman, and Dritzhen also provided money to fund the work. At the end of five years, the men would share whatever profits they had made.
You write out the terms of our contract and each of us will sign.
To keep our partnership secret, we must work separately. We should not be seen together or people may discover our plans.
While his three partners were busy working elsewhere, Gutenberg experimented with ink and paper.
The linseed oil, soot, and amber must be mixed in exactly the right amount. The paper must be soft enough to accept the ink.
But paper that is too soft will make the ink run. The letters then are not sharp and clear.

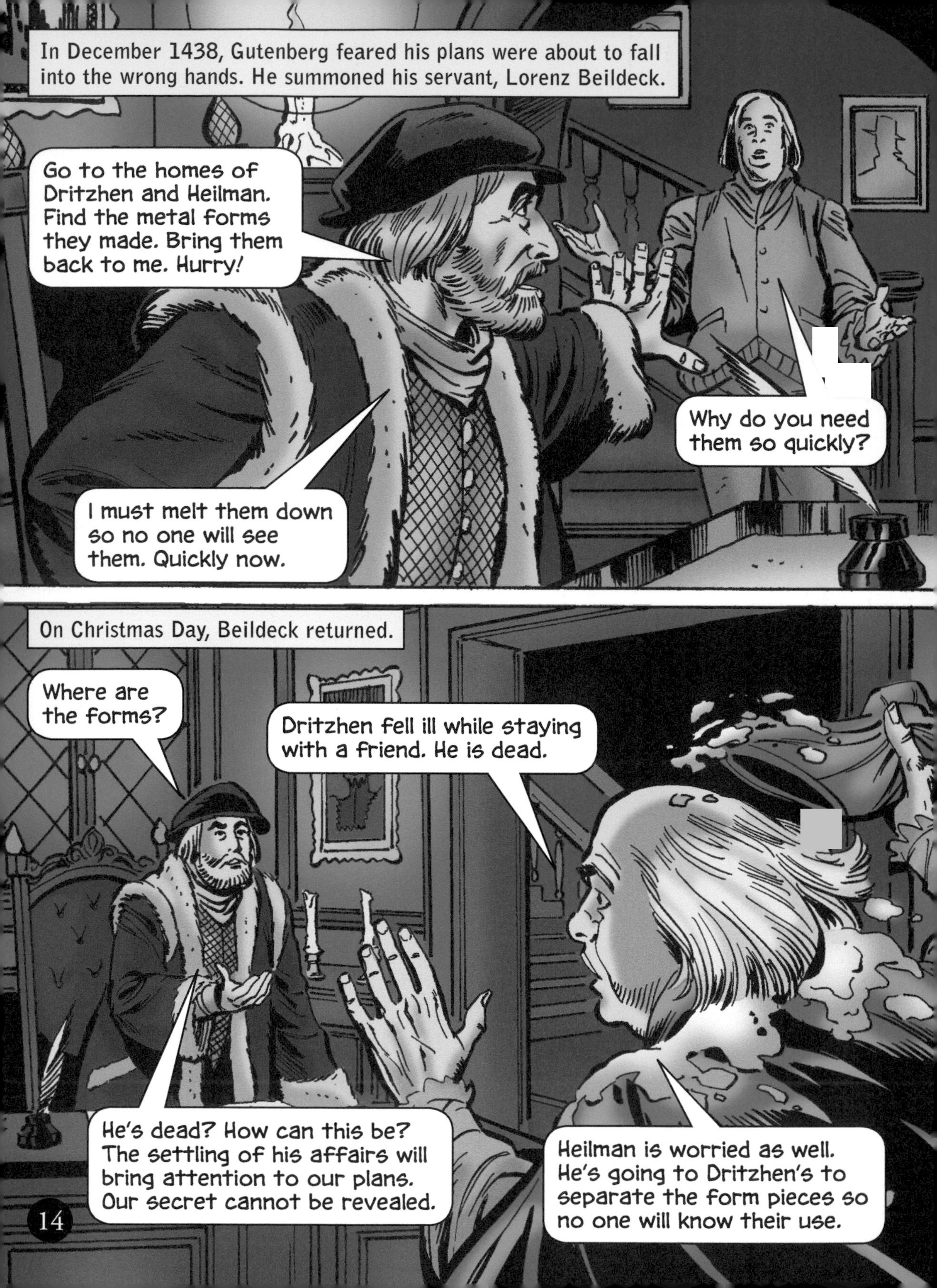
In December 1438, Gutenberg feared his plans were about to fall into the wrong hands. He summoned his servant, Lorenz Beildeck.
Go to the homes of Dritzhen and Heilman. Find the metal forms they made. Bring them back to me. Hurry!
Why do you need them so quickly?
I must melt them down so no one will see them. Quickly now.
On Christmas Day, Beildeck returned.
Where are the forms?
Dritzhen fell ill while staying with a friend. He is dead.
He's dead? How can this be? The settling of his affairs will bring attention to our plans. Our secret cannot be revealed.
Heilman is worried as well. He's going to Dritzhen's to separate the form pieces so no one will know their use.

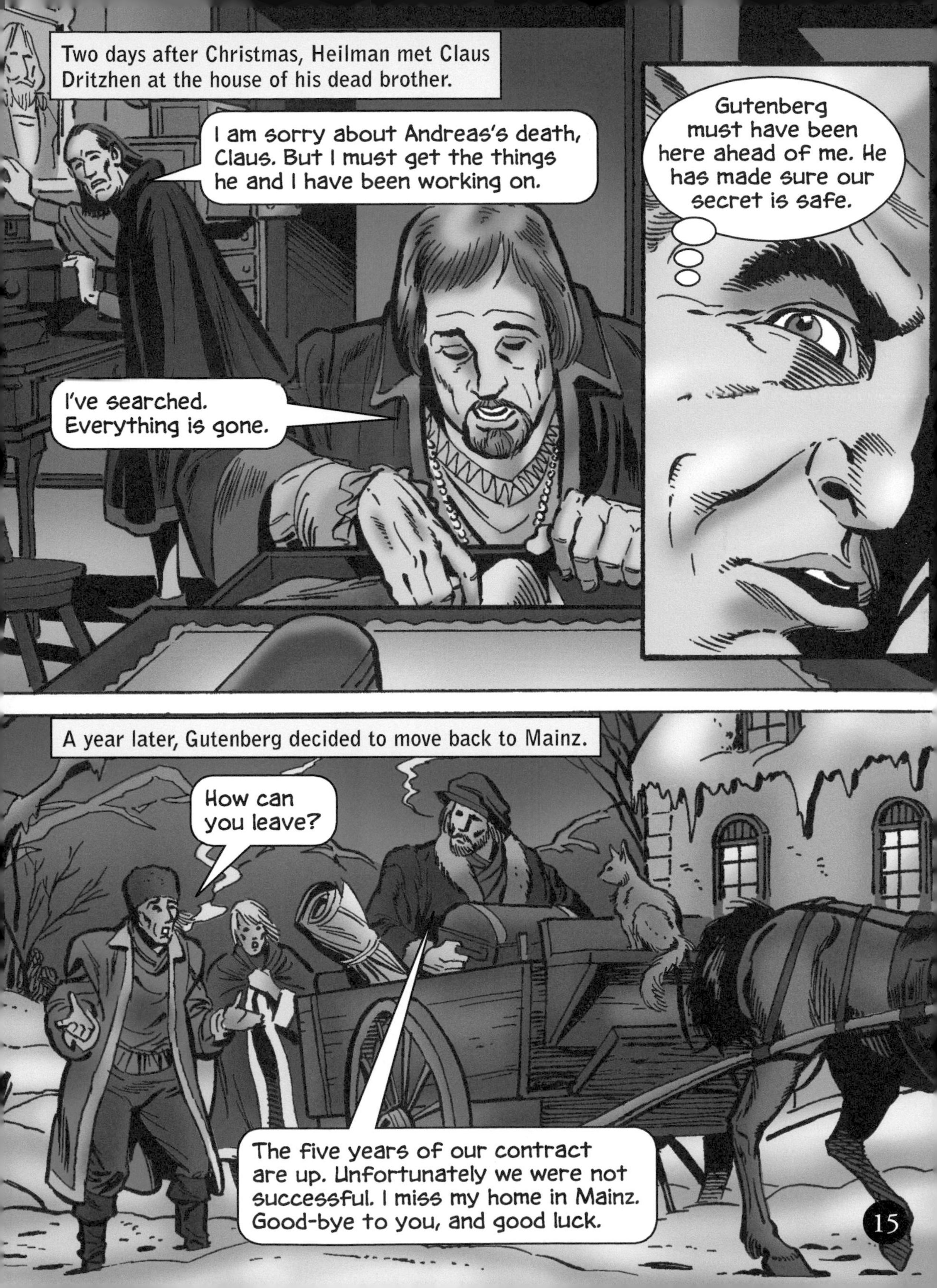
Two days after Christmas, Heilman met Claus Dritzhen at the house of his dead brother.
I am sorry about Andreas's death, Claus. But I must get the things he and I have been working on.
I've searched. Everything is gone.
Gutenberg must have been here ahead of me. He has made sure our secret is safe.
A year later, Gutenberg decided to move back to Mainz.
How can you leave?
The five years of our contract are up. Unfortunately we were not successful. I miss my home in Mainz. Good-bye to you, and good luck.

Chapter 3

The Printing Press

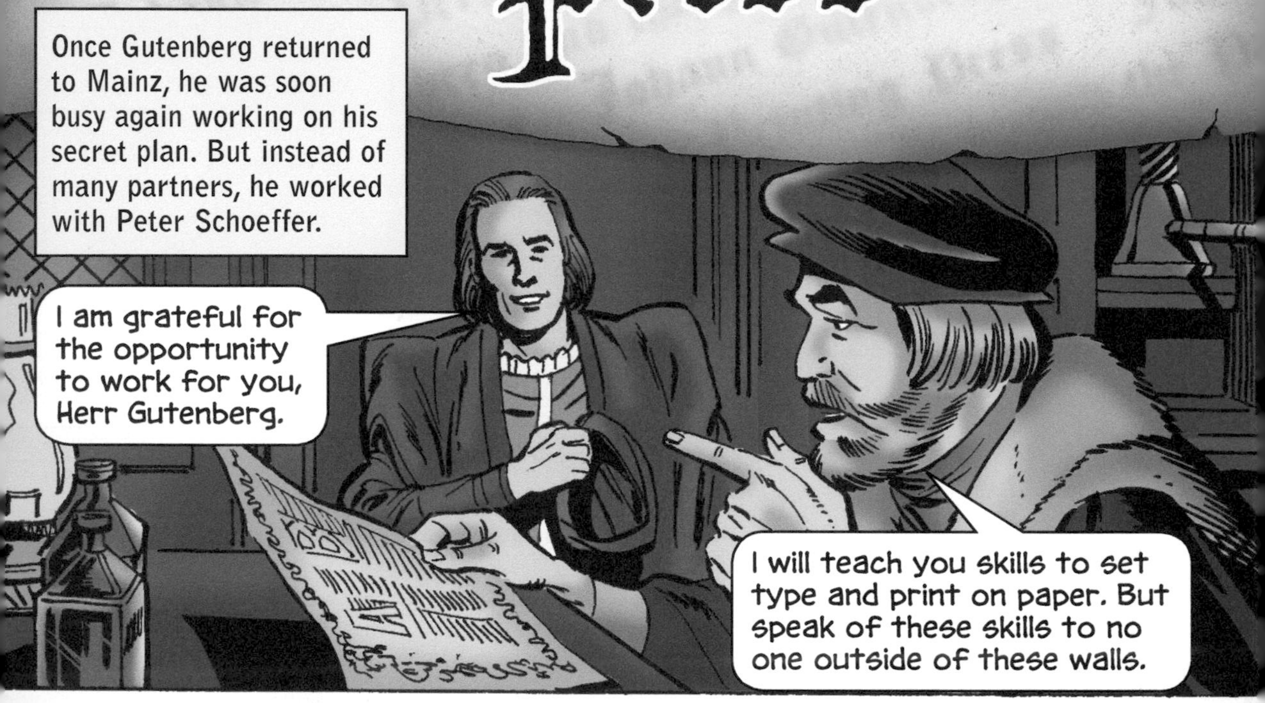
Once Gutenberg returned to Mainz, he was soon busy again working on his secret plan. But instead of many partners, he worked with Peter Schoeffer.
I am grateful for the opportunity to work for you, Herr Gutenberg.
I will teach you skills to set type and print on paper. But speak of these skills to no one outside of these walls.

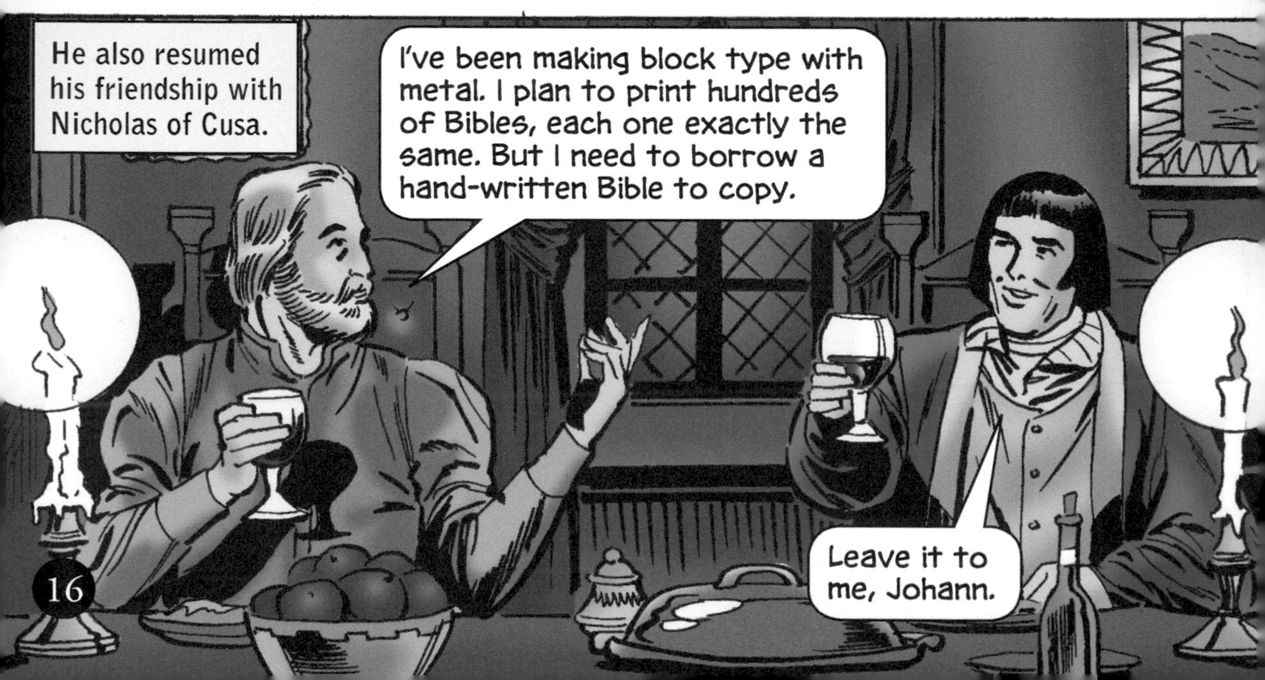
He also resumed his friendship with Nicholas of Cusa.
I've been making block type with metal. I plan to print hundreds of Bibles, each one exactly the same. But I need to borrow a hand-written Bible to copy.
Leave it to me, Johann.

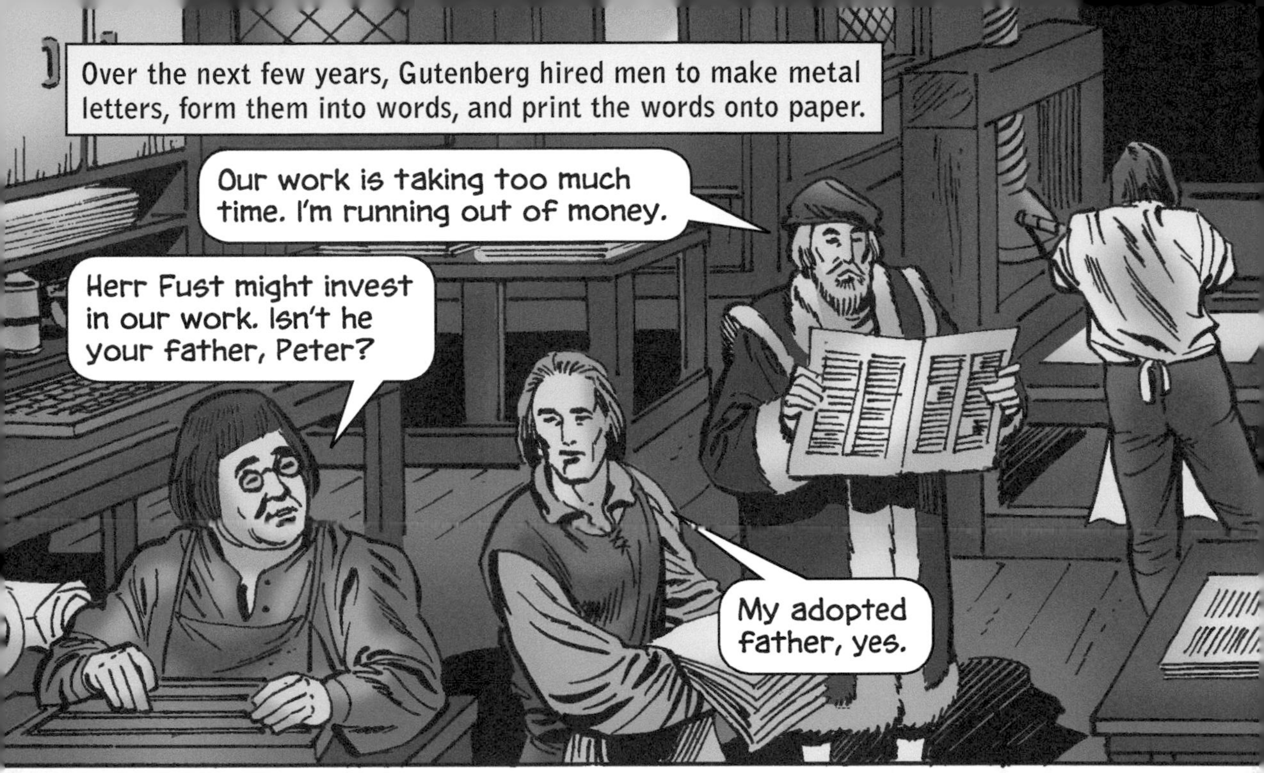
Over the next few years, Gutenberg hired men to make metal letters, form them into words, and print the words onto paper.
Our work is taking too much time. I'm running out of money.
Herr Fust might invest in our work. Isn't he your father, Peter?
My adopted father, yes.

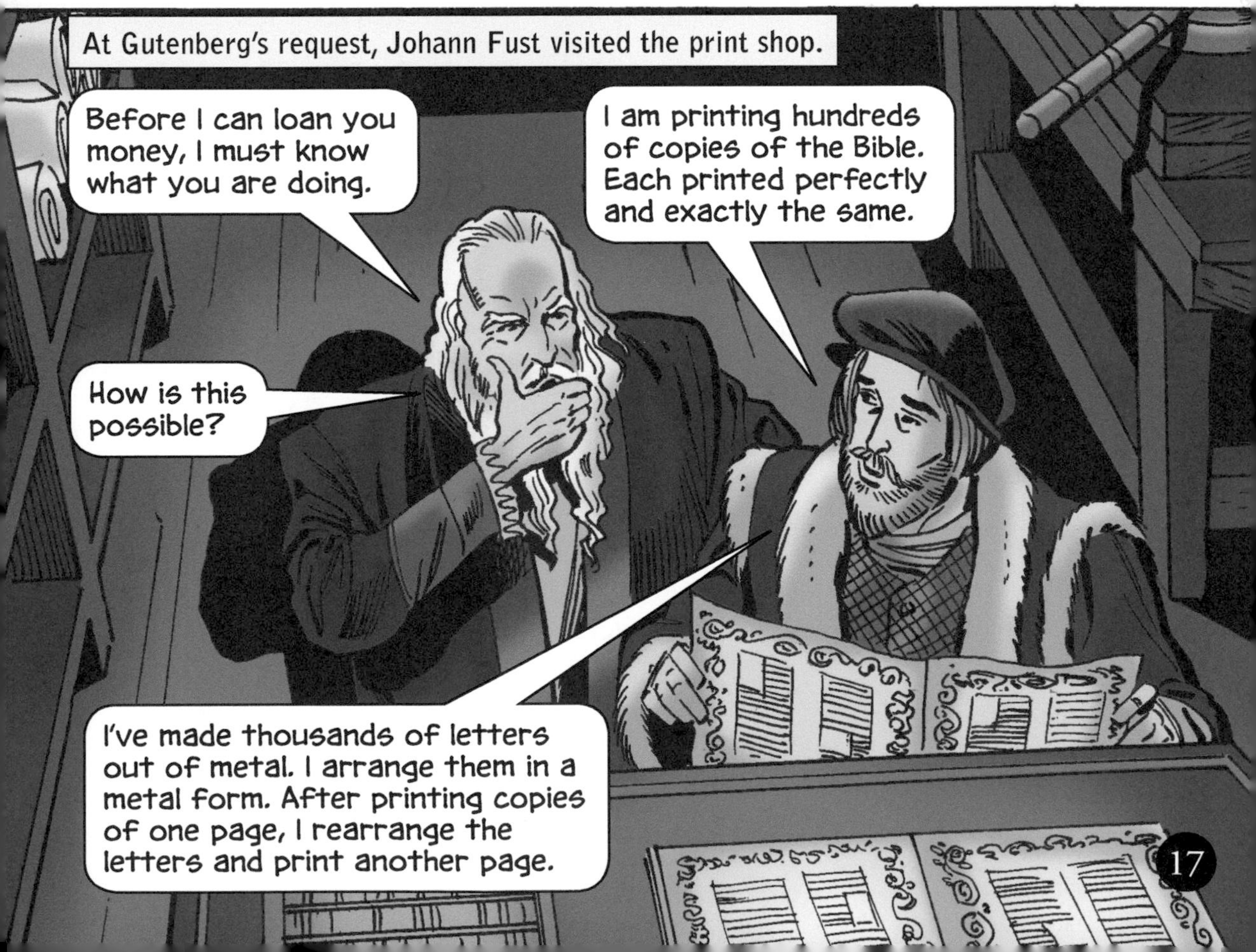
At Gutenberg's request, Johann Fust visited the print shop.
Before I can loan you money, I must know what you are doing.
I am printing hundreds of copies of the Bible. Each printed perfectly and exactly the same.
How is this possible?
I've made thousands of letters out of metal. I arrange them in a metal form. After printing copies of one page, I rearrange the letters and print another page.

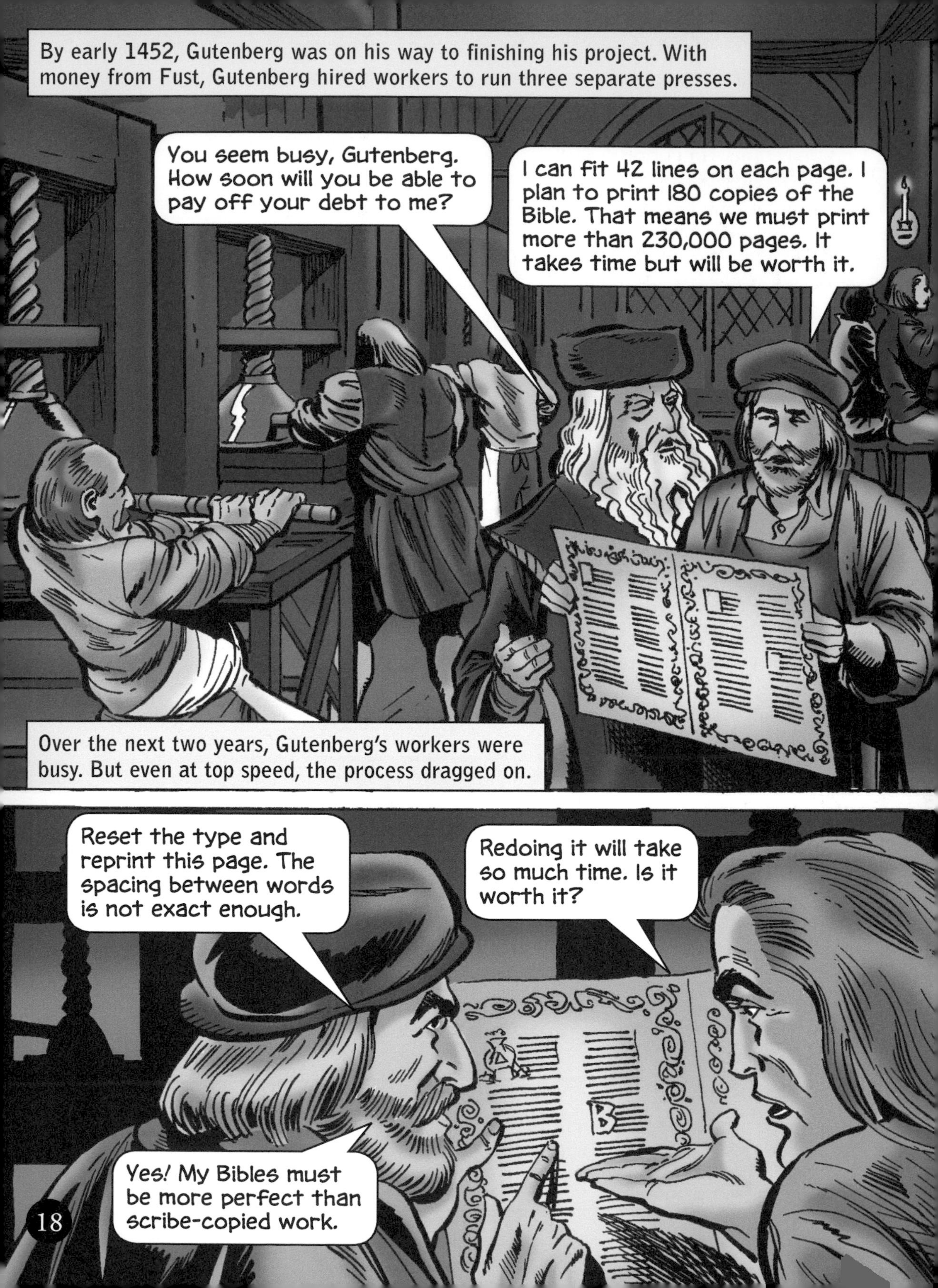
By early 1452, Gutenberg was on his way to finishing his project. With money from Fust, Gutenberg hired workers to run three separate presses.
You seem busy, Gutenberg. How soon will you be able to pay off your debt to me?
I can fit 42 lines on each page. I plan to print 180 copies of the Bible. That means we must print more than 230,000 pages. It takes time but will be worth it.
Over the next two years, Gutenberg's workers were busy. But even at top speed, the process dragged on.
Reset the type and reprint this page. The spacing between words is not exact enough.
Redoing it will take so much time. Is it worth it?
Yes! My Bibles must be more perfect than scribe-copied work.

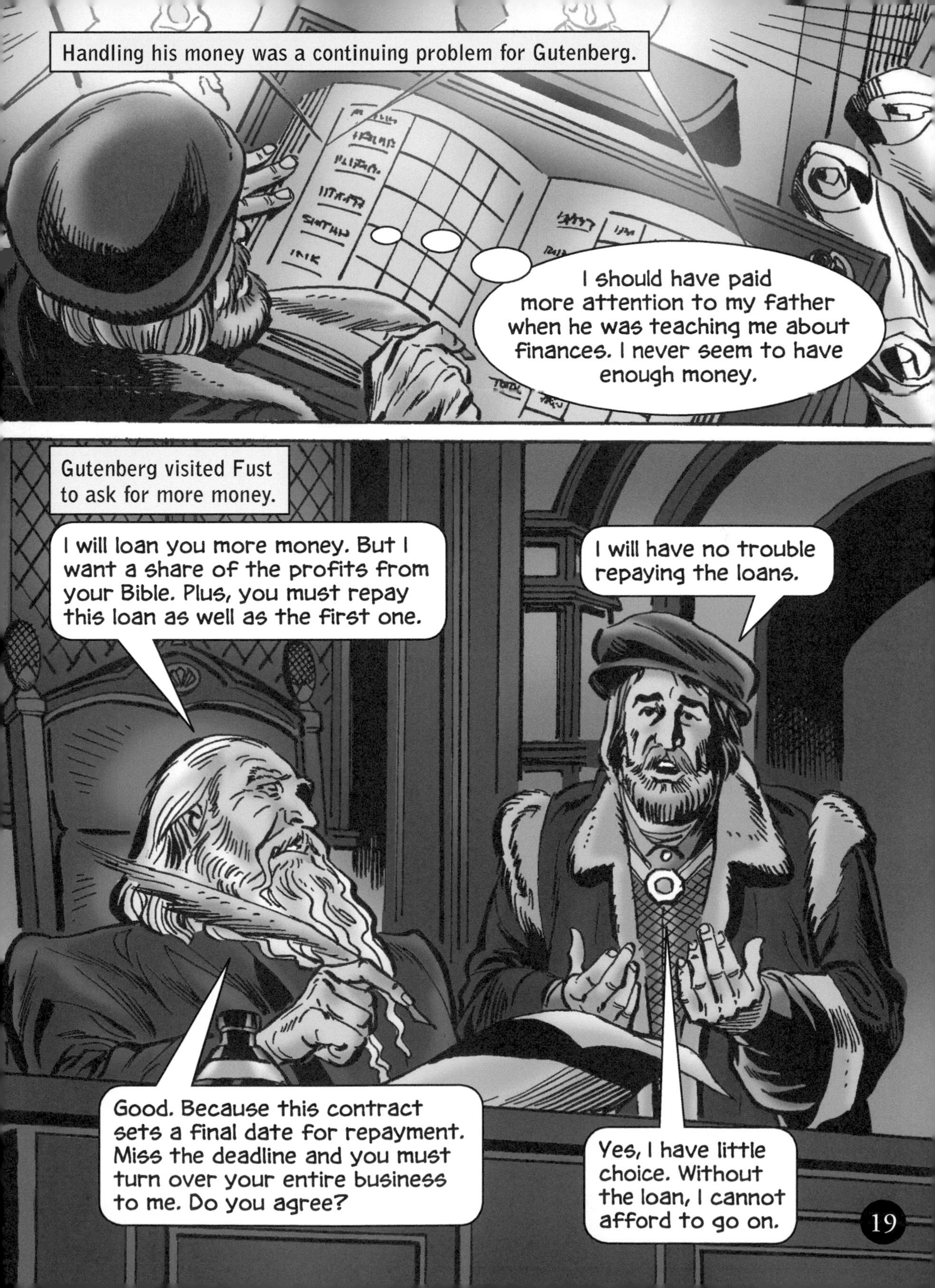
Handling his money was a continuing problem for Gutenberg.
I should have paid more attention to my father when he was teaching me about finances. I never seem to have enough money.
Gutenberg visited Fust to ask for more money.
I will loan you more money. But I want a share of the profits from your Bible. Plus, you must repay this loan as well as the first one.
I will have no trouble repaying the loans.
Good. Because this contract sets a final date for repayment. Miss the deadline and you must turn over your entire business to me. Do you agree?
Yes, I have little choice. Without the loan, I cannot afford to go on.

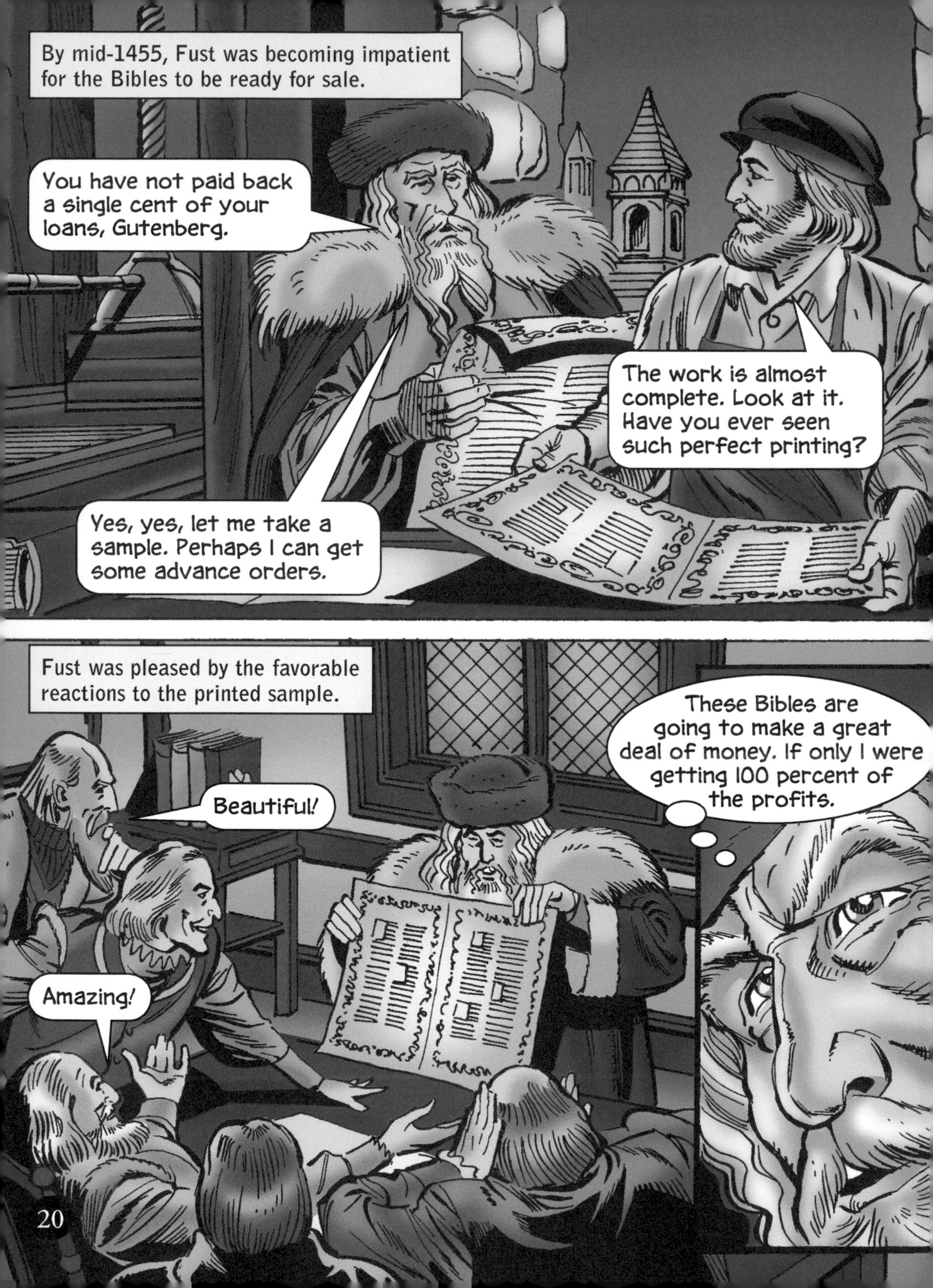
By mid-1455, Fust was becoming impatient for the Bibles to be ready for sale.
You have not paid back a single cent of your loans, Gutenberg.
The work is almost complete. Look at it. Have you ever seen such perfect printing?
Yes, yes, let me take a sample. Perhaps I can get some advance orders.
Fust was pleased by the favorable reactions to the printed sample.
Beautiful!
Amazing!
These Bibles are going to make a great deal of money. If only I were getting 100 percent of the profits.

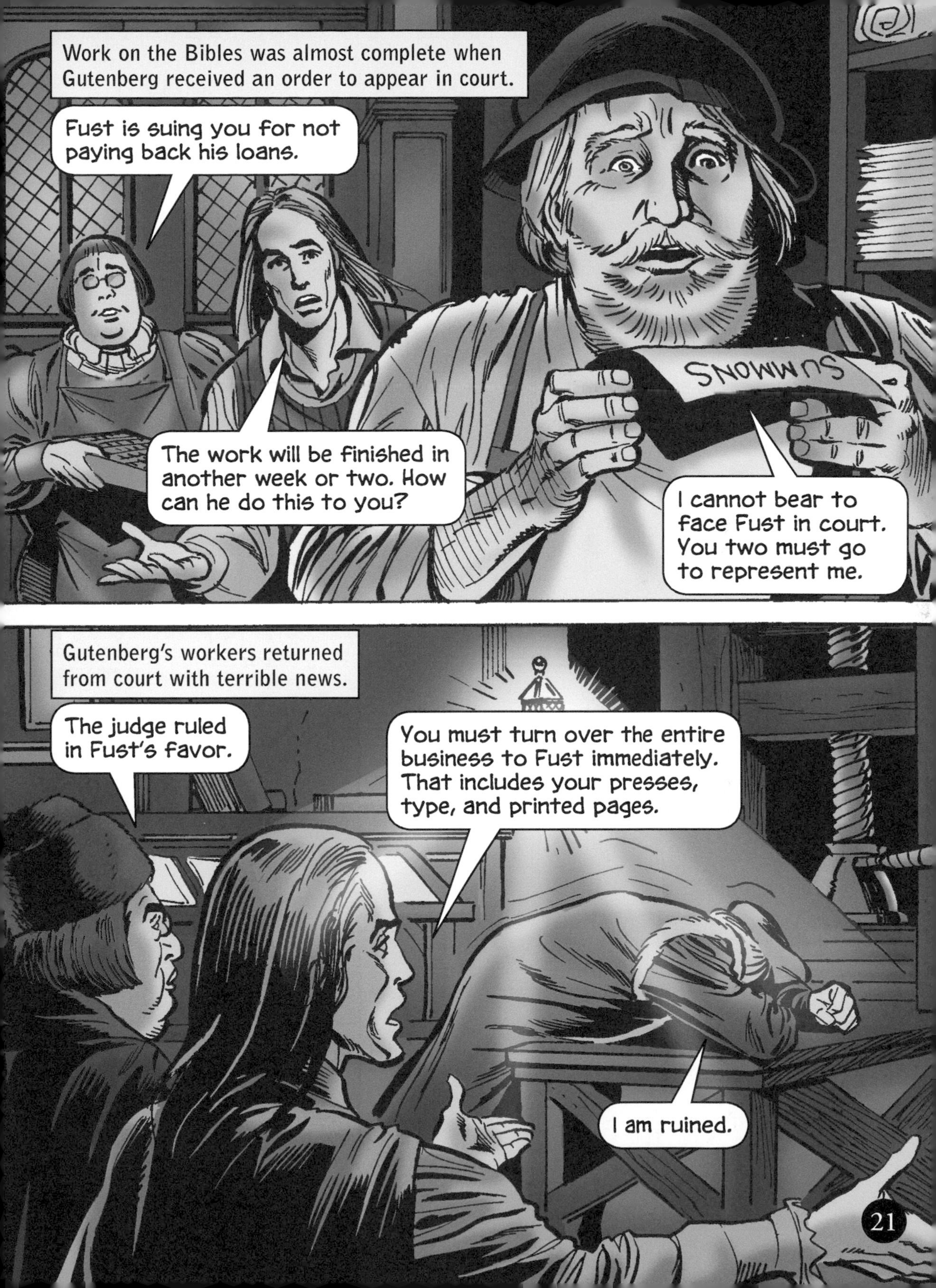
Work on the Bibles was almost complete when Gutenberg received an order to appear in court.
Fust is suing you for not paying back his loans.
The work will be finished in another week or two. How can he do this to you?
SUMMONS
I cannot bear to face Fust in court. You two must go to represent me.
Gutenberg's workers returned from court with terrible news.
The judge ruled in Fust's favor.
You must turn over the entire business to Fust immediately. That includes your presses, type, and printed pages.
I am ruined.

Chapter 4 The Printing Business

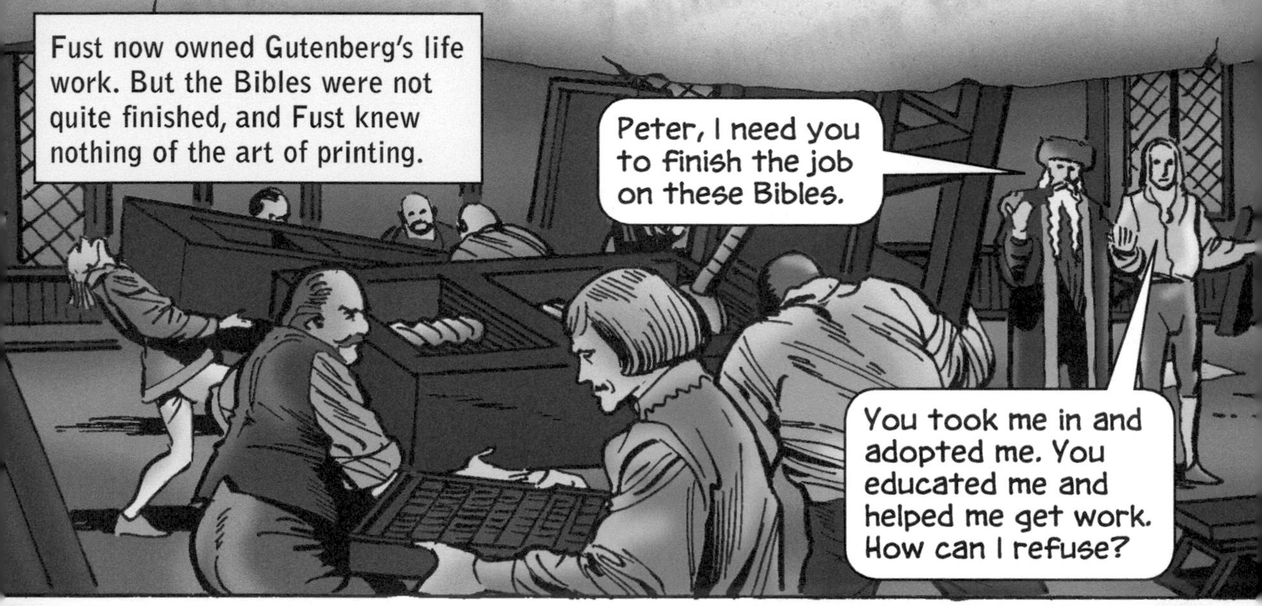
Fust now owned Gutenberg's life work. But the Bibles were not quite finished, and Fust knew nothing of the art of printing.
Peter, I need you to finish the job on these Bibles.
You took me in and adopted me. You educated me and helped me get work. How can I refuse?

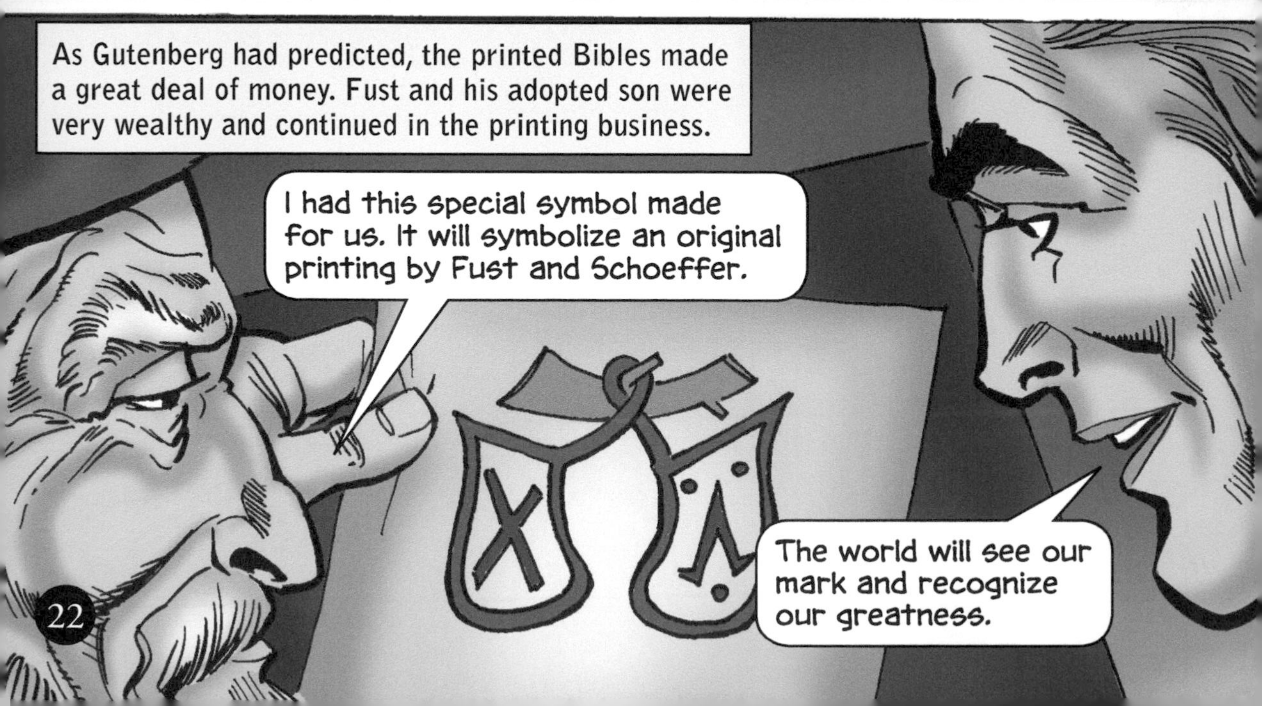
As Gutenberg had predicted, the printed Bibles made a great deal of money. Fust and his adopted son were very wealthy and continued in the printing business.
I had this special symbol made for us. It will symbolize an original printing by Fust and Schoeffer.
The world will see our mark and recognize our greatness.

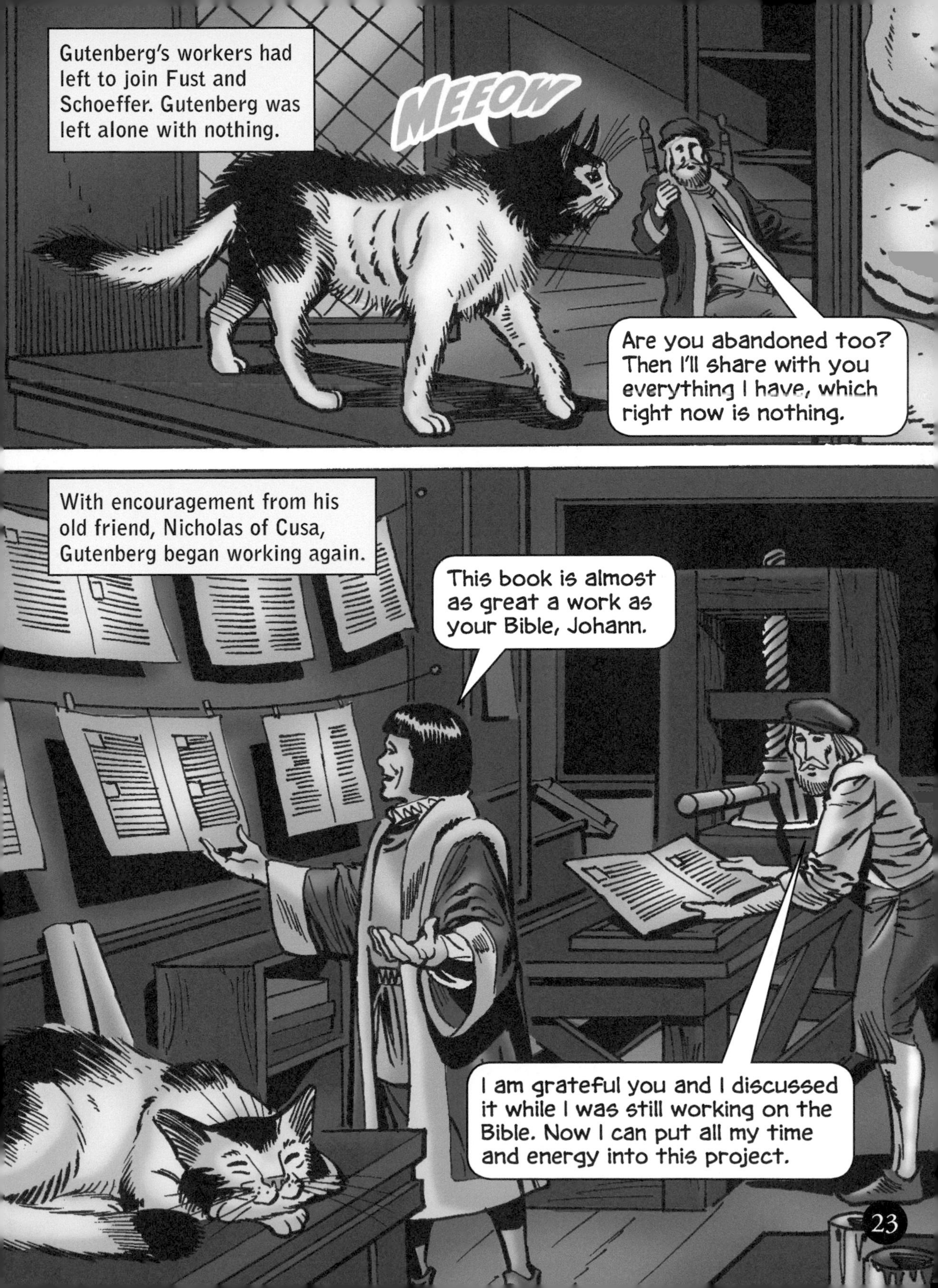
Gutenberg's workers had left to join Fust and Schoeffer. Gutenberg was left alone with nothing.
MEEOW
Are you abandoned too? Then I'll share with you everything I have, which right now is nothing.
With encouragement from his old friend, Nicholas of Cusa, Gutenberg began working again.
This book is almost as great a work as your Bible, Johann.
I am grateful you and I discussed it while I was still working on the Bible. Now I can put all my time and energy into this project.

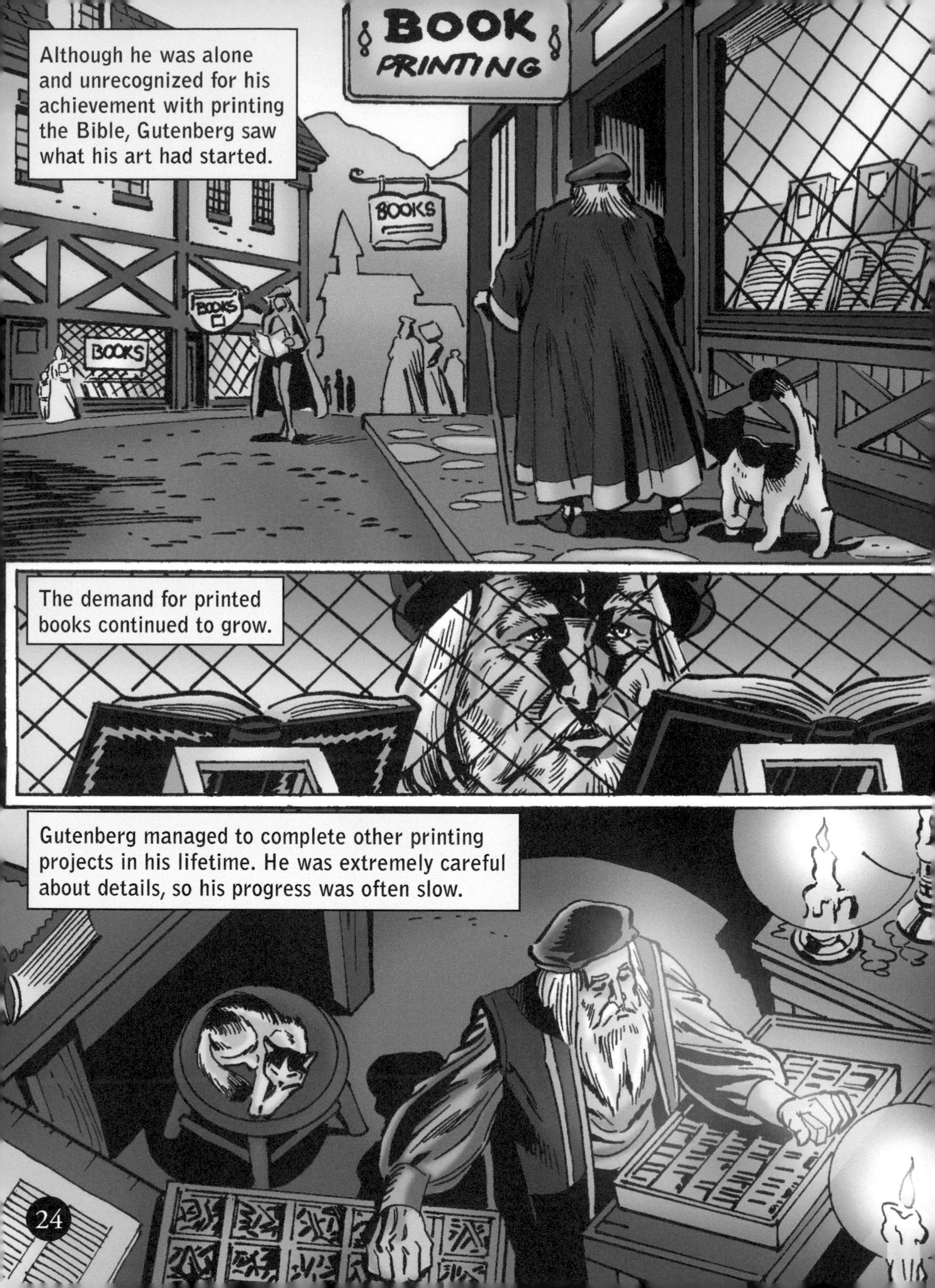
Although he was alone and unrecognized for his achievement with printing the Bible, Gutenberg saw what his art had started.
BOOK PRINTING
BOOKS
BOOKS
BOOKS
The demand for printed books continued to grow.
Gutenberg managed to complete other printing projects in his lifetime. He was extremely careful about details, so his progress was often slow.

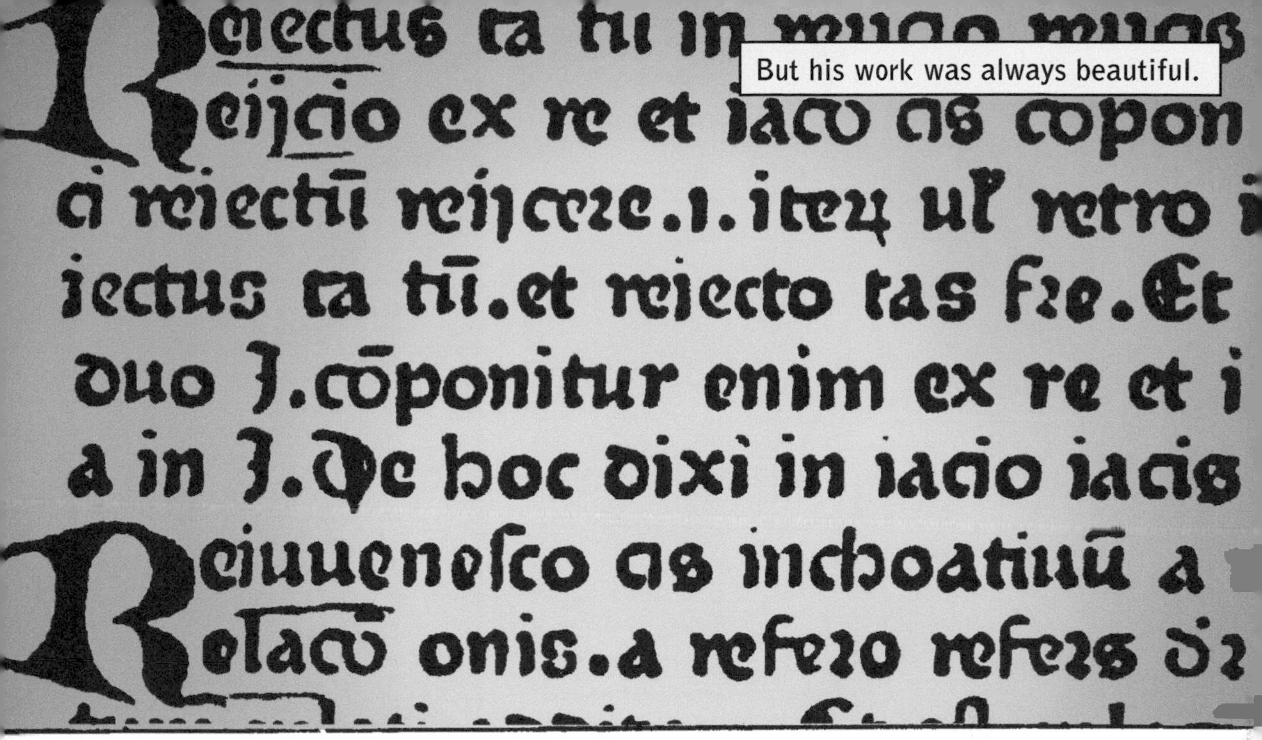
But his work was always beautiful.

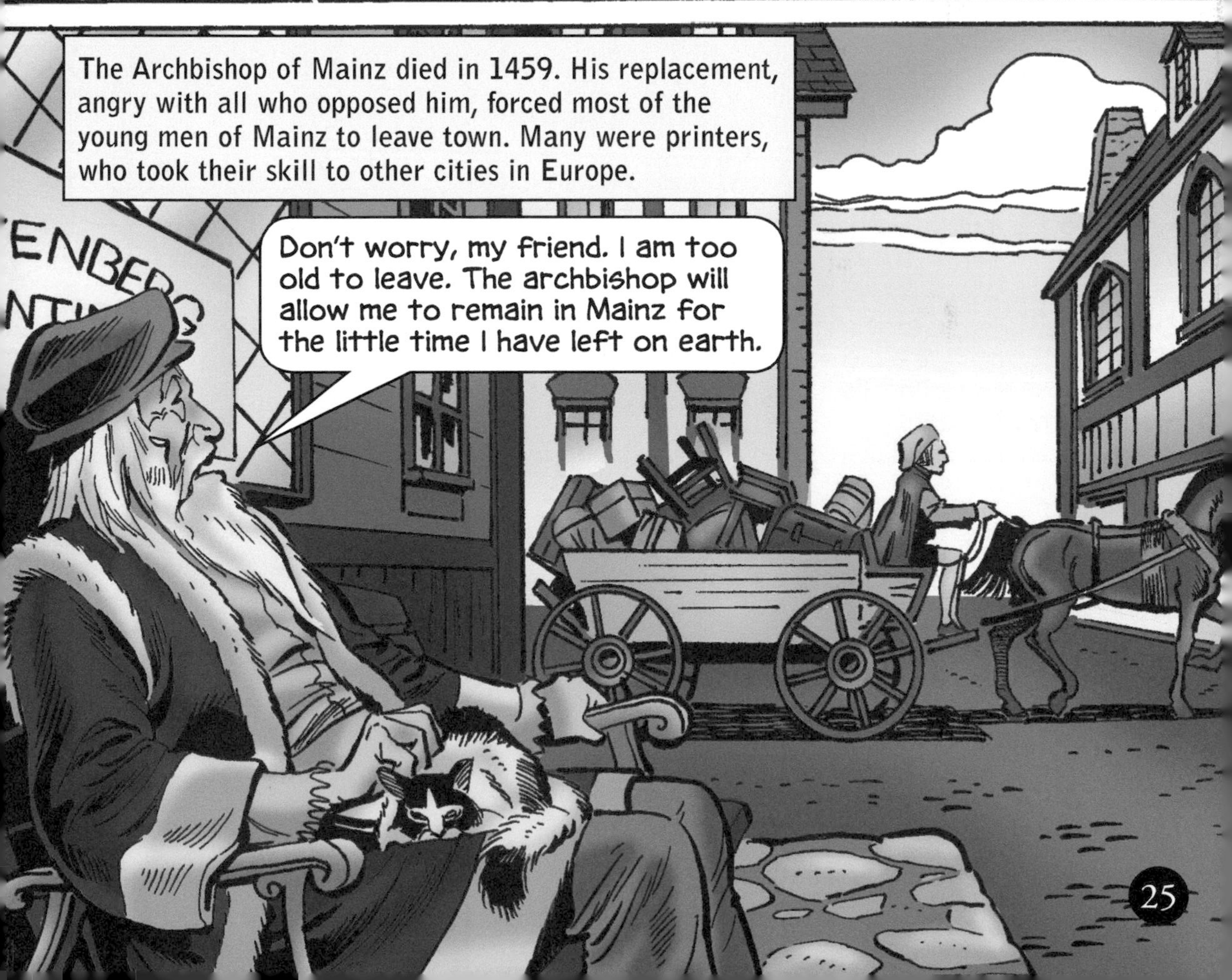
The Archbishop of Mainz died in 1459. His replacement, angry with all who opposed him, forced most of the young men of Mainz to leave town. Many were printers, who took their skill to other cities in Europe.
Don't worry, my friend. I am too old to leave. The archbishop will allow me to remain in Mainz for the little time I have left on earth.

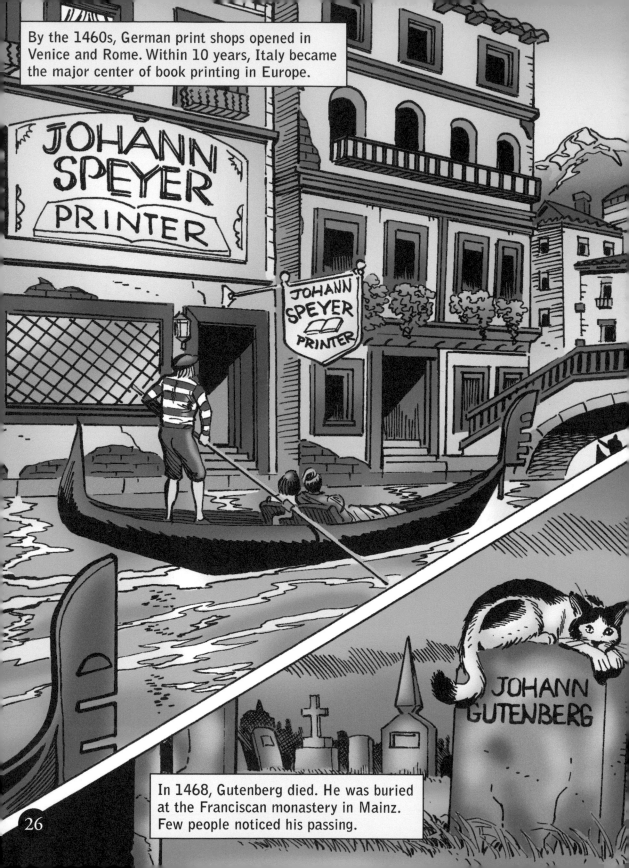

By the 1460s, German print shops opened in Venice and Rome. Within 10 years, Italy became the major center of book printing in Europe.

JOHANN SPEYER PRINTER

JOHANN SPEYER PRINTER

In 1468, Gutenberg died. He was buried at the Franciscan monastery in Mainz. Few people noticed his passing.

JOHANN GUTENBERG

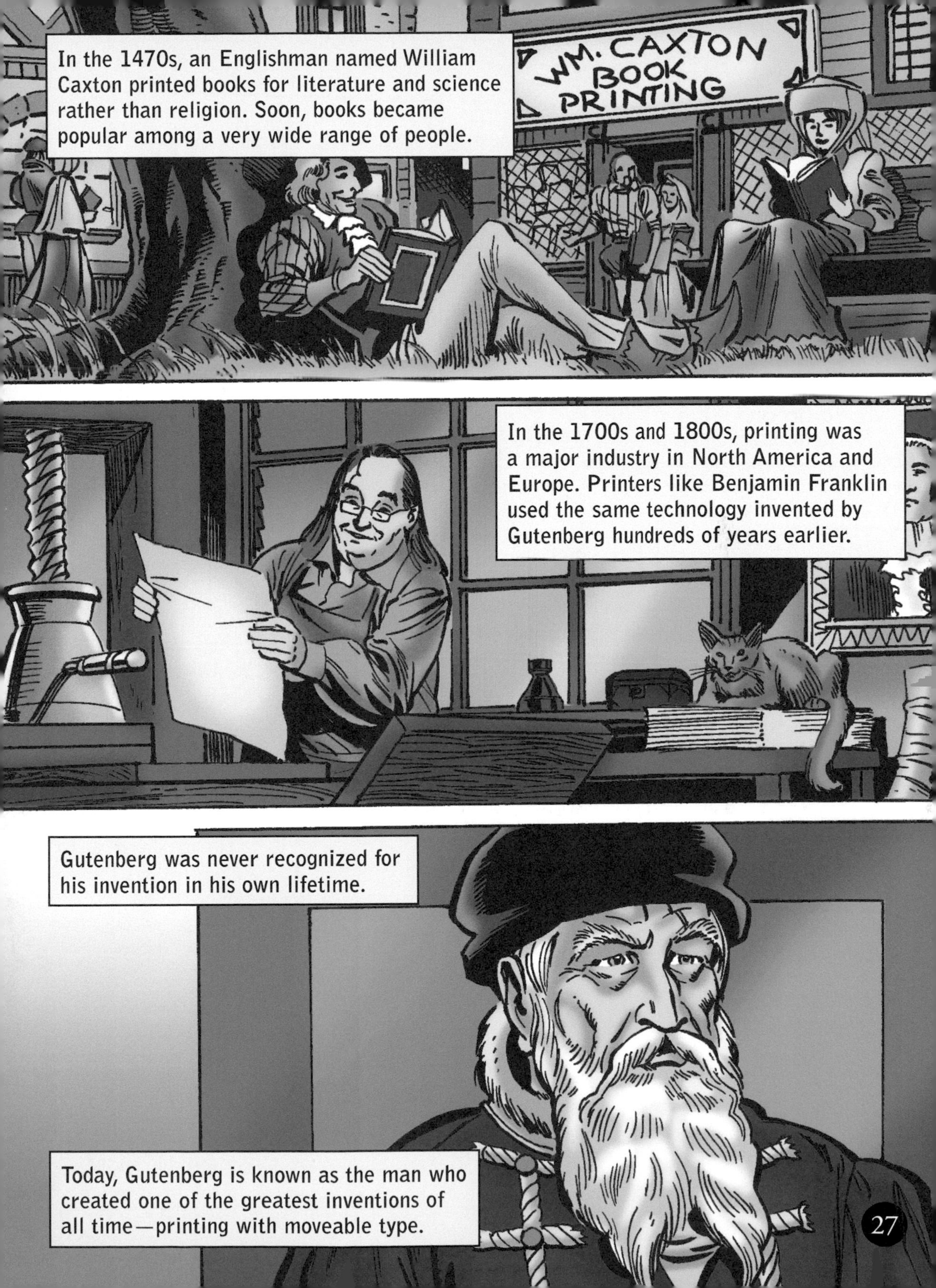
In the 1470s, an Englishman named William Caxton printed books for literature and science rather than religion. Soon, books became popular among a very wide range of people.
WM. CAXTON BOOK PRINTING
In the 1700s and 1800s, printing was a major industry in North America and Europe. Printers like Benjamin Franklin used the same technology invented by Gutenberg hundreds of years earlier.
Gutenberg was never recognized for his invention in his own lifetime.
Today, Gutenberg is known as the man who created one of the greatest inventions of all time—printing with moveable type.

Johann Gutenberg and the Printing Press

Little is known about Johann Gutenberg. He was born in Mainz, Germany, around 1397, but no one knows the exact date. Gutenberg's father was named Friele and his mother was Else. Johann grew up with his parents, one brother, and one sister.

Nicholas of Cusa was born in 1401 and was about three years younger than Gutenberg. Nicholas became a lawyer and important church leader. In February 1432, Nicholas was sent to Mainz on business. It is possible that he and Gutenberg met at that time, but no one knows for sure.

The genius of Gutenberg's art was the metal type he made. Each letter was exactly the same height as all the others, so the printing would be even. Blank pieces were made to fit between words. Each line of type fit exactly into the form. Gutenberg was very particular and insisted that each page be absolutely perfect.

Gutenberg kept his metal letters in drawers called cases. Each case had dividers to keep all the different letters separate. He kept the capital letters in the upper case and small letters in the lower case. Even today, capital letters are known as "uppercase" letters and small letters are called "lowercase" letters.

When he started printing the pages of the Bible, Gutenberg had two columns of print on each page with 40 lines in each column. As his costs grew, Gutenberg decided to save on paper by putting 42 lines in each column. He printed the rest of the Bible pages with two columns of 42 lines each. Original Gutenberg Bibles are known as the 42-line Bible, even though some pages have columns with only 40 lines.

Of the nearly 200 Bibles Gutenberg printed, only 48 still exist today. But recent technology has made it easier than ever for anyone to view this priceless book. Digital copies are now available, allowing the general public to see all 1,282 pages on their computers.

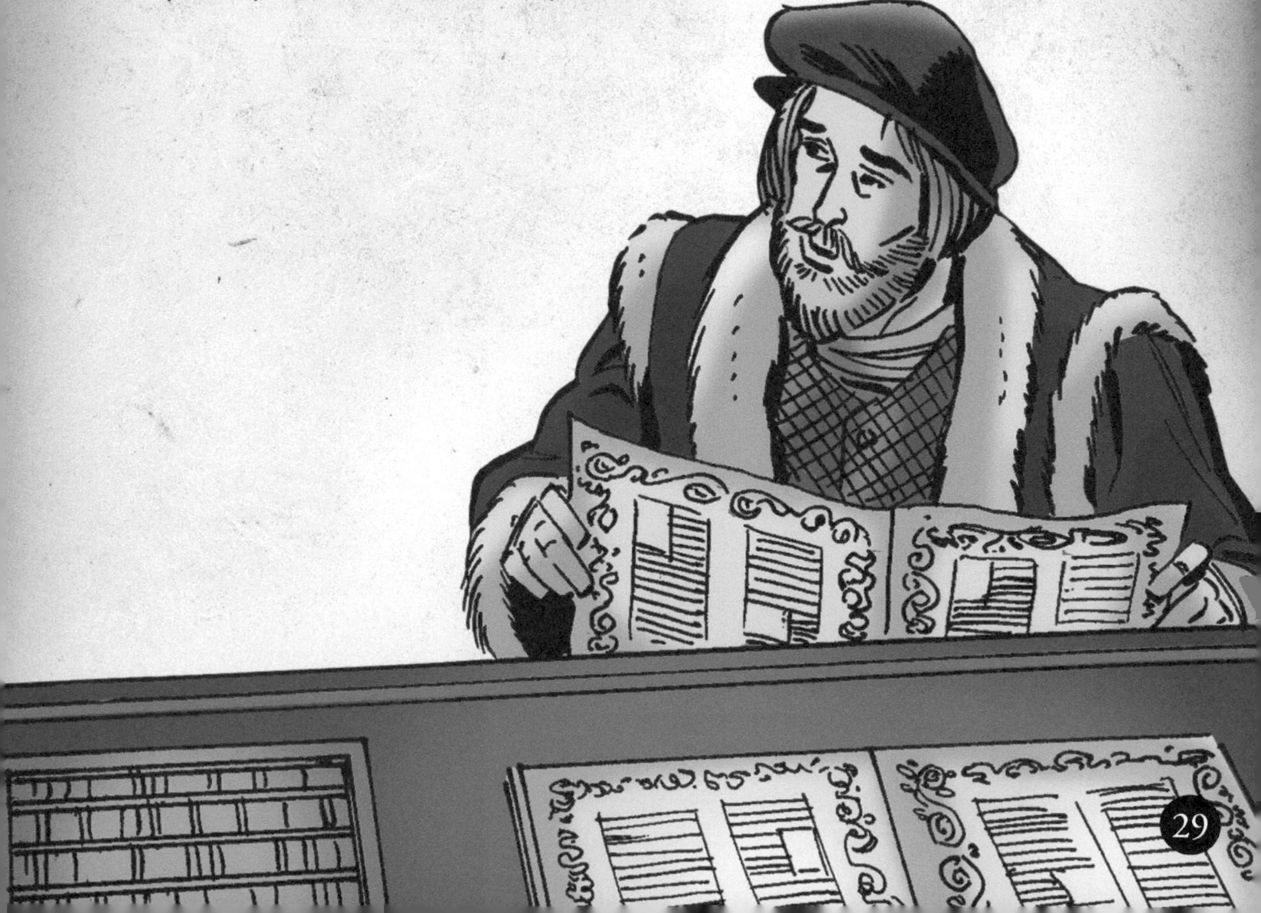

Glossary

engrave (en-GRAYV)—to cut a design or letters into a metal, wood, or glass surface

monastery (MON-uh-ster-ee)—a group of buildings where monks live and work

novice (NOV-iss)—someone who joins a religious order for a trial period before taking vows

scribe (SKRIBE)—a person who copies books, letters, contracts, and other documents by hand

scriptorium (skrip-TOR-ee-uhm)—a copying room for scribes

vellum (VEL-uhm)—fine parchment paper made from the skin of a calf, lamb, or baby goat

Internet Sites

FactHound offers a safe, fun way to find Internet sites related to this book. All of the sites on FactHound have been researched by our staff.

Here's how:
1. Visit *www.facthound.com*
2. Choose your grade level.
3. Type in this book ID **0736864822** for age-appropriate sites. You may also browse subjects by clicking on letters, or by clicking on pictures and words.
4. Click on the **Fetch It** button.

FactHound will fetch the best sites for you!

Read More

Koscielniak, Bruce. *Johann Gutenberg and the Amazing Printing Press.* Boston: Houghton Mifflin, 2003.

Pollard, Michael. *Johann Gutenberg: Master of Modern Printing.* Giants of Science. Woodbridge, Conn.: Blackbirch Press, 2001.

Rees, Fran. *Johannes Gutenberg: Inventor of the Printing Press.* Signature Lives. Minneapolis: Compass Point Books, 2006.

Bibliography

Gutenberg Homepage. http://www.gutenberg.de/english/

Ing, Janet Thompson. *Johann Gutenberg and His Bible: A Historical Study.* New York: Typophiles, 1988.

Kapr, Albert. *Johann Gutenberg: The Man and His Invention.* Aldershot, England; Brookfield, Vt.: Scolar Press, 1996.

Man, John. *Gutenberg: How One Man Remade the World with Words.* New York: John Wiley & Sons, 2002.

University of Texas at Austin. *Gutenberg Bible at the Ransom Center.* Harry Ransom Center Online Exibition http://www.hrc.utexas.edu/exhibitions/permanent/gutenberg/

Index